Mom's Pocket Guide
to Watching
FOOTBALL

Mom's Pocket Guide to Watching FOOTBALL

LINDA WONG AND
KAILEE WONG

Library of Congress Cataloging-in-Publication Data available upon request from publisher.

ISBN: 1-57500-149-7

Photo of Linda and Kailee by David Hansen, Houston, Texas.

The publisher has made every effort to secure permission to reproduce copyrighted material and would like to apologize should there have been any errors or omissions.

TV Books, L.L.C.
1619 Broadway, Ninth Floor
New York, NY 10019
www.tvbooks.com

Interior design by Deborah Daly
Illustrations by Kersti Frigell
MANUFACTURED IN CANADA

ACKNOWLEDGMENTS

Appreciation is extended to my sister, Kathryn Spiess, who planted the seed for this book by emphasizing (and demonstrating) the need for a basic football book for women. Appreciation is also extended to Mike Jodoin, Kailee's former football coach at North Eugene High School, for his feedback and support; to Steve Baker, NFL agent, who has been instrumental in multiple phases of this book; and to Warren Cowan of Warren Cowan Associates for guiding us to our literary agent, Alan Nevins. Alan Nevins, from AMG/Renaissance, became the bridge between the manuscript and our publisher. I am very grateful to Kailee for the wonderful experiences we shared in the process of writing this book as well as the experiences shared throughout his years of growing up. Both Kailee and I wish to express our appreciation to Albert DePetrillo, Rebecca McKenna, and TV Books for their interest and support in publishing this book. A venture such as this takes teamwork, and we are proud to be members of a well-orchestrated team!

—*Linda Wong*

INTRODUCTION

I am so glad that Mom and I were able to write this book for you. I want you to believe something that I believe: none of your questions about football are "dumb questions." Until recently, women weren't allowed to play football, so they haven't had the advantage or the experience of learning the game by playing the game. Oftentimes it is difficult to learn something without firsthand experience. The alternative is to ask questions, lots of questions. Many of the little nuances of football are learned best by asking questions. Hopefully, many of your questions are answered in this book. Now you can support your favorite players and let your voices be heard from the stands! Thank you for wanting to learn!

—Kailee Wong

The talent, skills, strategies, and devotion required to play football are analogous to a game of chess, a musical composition, a fine piece of art, or a dance form such as ballet. People can enjoy a game of chess without being experts; however, the more they learn, the more intriguing the game becomes. People can enjoy the beauty of music without knowing personally how to compose, read sheet music, sing notes, or even play an instrument. People can appreciate a fine work of art or become ballet enthusiasts without knowing how to daub oils on a canvas or perform a perfect plié. I think you get the point. In football, as in so many things in life, there will always be those who masterfully create and perform, and there will always be those who assume the role of the enthusiastic spectators.

This book is your guide to becoming an informed, enthusiastic spectator! If you are interested and eager to learn, *Mom's Pocket Guide to Watching Football* is your opportunity to cease being the confused spectator, the frustrated "football widow," or the wishful mom who would like to understand more about her son's passion in life. Welcome to the exciting world of football!

—*Linda Wong*

CONTENTS

About This Book   11

Chapter 1: The Basics   15
  A. The Object of the Game   17
  B. The Field   18
  C. The Teams   21
  D. The Line of Scrimmage   28
  E. The Downs   30
  F. The Chains   32
  G. The Fourth Down   34
  H. The Length of the Game   36
  I. The Kick Off   40
  J. The Action Continues   44

Chapter 2: Scoring Points   45

  A. Touchdown   47
  B. Point After   48
  C. Two-Point Conversion   49
  D. Field Goal   50
  E. Safety   51

Chapter 3: Offensive Players   52
  A. Basic Offensive Formation   53
  B. The Quarterback   56
  C. The Center   63
  D. Two Guards and Two Tackles   65
  E. The Wide Receivers   68
  F. The Tight End   73
  G. The Running Backs   74

Chapter 4: Defensive Players   79
  A. Basic Defensive Formation   80
  B. The Defensive Linemen   83
  C. The Linebackers   86
  D. Basics about the Secondary   90
  E. The Cornerbacks   93
  F. The Safeties   94

Chapter 5: Special Teams   97
  A. The Kick Off Team   98
  B. The Kick Off Return Team   101
  C. The Punt Team   104
  D. The Punt Return Team   109
  E. The PAT Kicking Team   112
  F. The PAT Blocking Team   117

Chapter 6: Common Penalties   118
  A. Common Terms   119
  B. Common Penalties   121

Chapter 7: Tips and Final Thoughts   132

Glossary of Common Terms   141

ABOUT THIS BOOK

This book is designed to simplify the complex game of football. Once Kailee and I decided to write a football book for women, we spent a considerable amount of time discussing the most interesting, direct, and comprehensible way to present the information. Our goal was to limit the discussion to the basics and to provide a solid foundation of understanding for readers who want to understand and enjoy the game.

To add extra interest to the book, we decided to share a little of our personal lives and stories with you. These numerous anecdotes which I have collected over the years appear in italics. Some of the anecdotes are interesting questions I have heard women pose; some were specific questions posed by my younger sister, Kathryn, as she was learning to understand the action on the field. Other comments are my personal comments as a mother of a football player. We hope you enjoy these anecdotes.

As you will soon notice, each chapter focuses on one specific topic or aspect of football. In each chapter, you will see some words in bold print. These terms are defined in greater detail in the glossary at the end of the book. Your knowledge of football will continue to grow as you move from one chapter to another.

Chapter 1, "The Basics," provides you with an overview of the game. You'll learn about the object of the game, the field, and the teams. Basic terms such as downs, chains, fourth down, and the kick off will also be explained. After reading this chapter, you will already be off to a good start!

Chapter 2, "Scoring Points," will explain the five ways in which points can be scored. You'll understand the difference between touchdowns, points after, two-point conversions, field goals, and safeties. Once you learn the different types of points that can be scored, you'll be ready (and eager) to learn more about the players who put these points on the scoreboard.

Chapter 3, "Offensive Players," will provide you with information about basic offensive formations and individual offensive players. If you have someone special in your life who plays on the team's offense, you can learn about his basic position, his roles, and his responsibilities in the game. Of course, you'll also learn about his teammates, the other offensive players, and their functions and coordinated efforts to score points. With this information as a foundation, you will want to know more about the players the offensive team has to confront.

Chapter 4, "Defensive Players," introduces you to a basic defensive formation and defensive positions. You will become familiar with the roles and the responsibilities of the defensive linemen, the linebackers, and the players who comprise the "secondary." At this point, you'll be ready to learn about the "special teams."

Chapter 5, "Special Teams," introduces you to six different teams that are crucial in every football game. You'll learn about the teams that are involved in transition plays and teams that are on the field during kick offs.

Chapter 6, "Common Penalties," in a clear, concise manner explains common penalties called on players for different kinds of rule violations. When you hear a penalty called during the course of the game, you can quickly refer to this chapter for clarification.

Chapter 7, "Tips and Final Thoughts," provides you with some final thoughts and tips for attending games. Tips for mothers whose sons are playing ball and tips for players are included.

The Glossary of Terms at the end of the book provides you with another quick reference to use any time you hear a football term that you do not understand.

1
THE BASICS

Years ago, when I attended my first football game at the University of Oregon, I knew little about the game of football. To be honest, I knew *nothing!* I had grown up in Brazil, so I was much more familiar with soccer. I joined some friends for the Oregon Ducks game because I had just started dating one of the players. Well, I wondered about the ego of this man, when after the game he commented, "I'm so tired. I played the whole game." I was baffled. I had seen him go on and off the field many, many times. What I did not yet know is that football is not like soccer where the players stay on the field all the time with the exception of substitutions. I felt pretty silly later when I learned that he did indeed play the entire game and was on the field every time the offense was sent in. Oh, how I wish someone had given me a book on the basics of football! My learning would have been so much quicker and less painful and I would have been spared many embarrassing moments and feelings of ignorance.

Many years later, after Kailee had been born, had progressed through flag football, JV, and varsity football in high school, and was playing for Stanford, Kathryn, one of my younger sisters, came with me to a Stanford game, her first ever. Her questions were hysterical, but legitimate, and her desire to grasp the concepts of the game was real. After all, she wanted to know when to yell, cheer, jump up and down, and when to groan, wring her hands, and when to hold her breath on a crucial play. She wanted to understand the basic lingo. She wanted to know how many more minutes before "the break" so she could head to the restroom. She wanted to be able to appreciate the physical and mental skills of the players, the endurance they must develop, and the incredible coordination required to accomplish so many athletic feats. Thus, the idea for this book was born. After Kailee's career at Stanford ended and he finished his rookie year with the Minnesota Vikings, we started this joint project. He was surprised at how many things I knew, but also at how many things I did not know. So, now we share the basics of football with you. May your learning process be much quicker, direct, and successful than mine, which took more than a decade!

A. The Object of the Game

The object of football is simple: win the game by scoring the most points.

Two teams battle physically and mentally to make plays that result in points and to make plays that prevent the opponent from scoring points. Teams either battle to invade the other team's territory or to protect their own territory from invasion. This basic concept quickly becomes complex as coaches and players continually devise new plays, new formations, and new strategies to outsmart, outplay, and outscore the opponent.

As parents, sometimes we remind ourselves (and our kids) that the object of the game is not just about winning. We want our kids to have fun, to learn good sportsmanship skills, and to be team players. We want them to experience the thrill of victory and learn how to handle disappointments and defeats. Football, or any sport, does teach players valuable skills and lessons. However, as you might expect, when players of any sport move to higher levels, the object of the game becomes plain and simple: to win. The other benefits of playing are the "frosting on the cake."

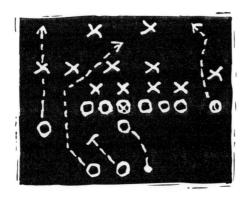

B. The Field

The field measures 160 feet wide and 100 yards long plus the ten yards on each end of the field which are termed the **end zones**; scoring takes place in the end zones. The zero yard line on each end of the field is called the **goal line**. The white lines across the field mark every five yards. The 50-yard line runs across the center of the field. As you move in either direction from the 50-yard line, you will see the 40-, 30-, 20-, and 10-yard line numbers marked on the field. The yard lines are referred to often to indicate where the ball is placed on the field. If you hear that the ball is on the "30-yard line," look to see which direction the team with the ball is moving.

Oh, I love the comments I hear at games! At a North Eugene High School game (Kailee's high school in Eugene, Oregon), a rather loud, obnoxious adult screamed for the team to "get in there and protect that !*@#?! red zone." A young girl behind me turned to her friend and asked, "Am I missing something? I don't see any red zone on the field. Does he know what he's screaming about?" By now the young lady is grown and most likely knows that a section of the field is not painted red. Young lady, if you are out there and still don't know what the red zone means, read on!

When the ball is within twenty yards from the end zone, the team with the ball is in the **red zone,** which means they are close to the end zone and well-positioned to score. The red zone is the danger zone for the defense, and an opportunity for the offense to score. The defense works extra hard to "defend the red zone" to prevent the other team from scoring. The offense sees the goal line and reaching the goal line seems more realistic. They are pumped to score.

The goalposts are ten yards behind the goal line. The lines at each end of the field where the goalposts are set are called the end lines. The end line at each end of the field and the sidelines that run down both sides of the field are the boundaries for the field. Any plays outside of the end lines or the sidelines are out of bounds and do not count.

The basics of the field are quite easy to understand once you know the meaning of the numbers, the lines, and the boundaries. The smaller lines, called hash marks, help keep the game and the beginning action of a play in the center part of the field. On one very cold, rainy football afternoon, when I was shivering in my boots and trying to keep the rain from seeping into my jacket, a lady next to me, a parent of one of the players, turned to me and asked, "I hope you don't mind this silly question, but I really want to know. Do players get penalized if they step on the short lines in the middle of the field?" A little stunned by her question, I stopped worrying about the rain and tried looking her straight in the eye without laughing. I wanted to ask her if she thought football was like a game of hopscotch! However, not wanting to be rude, I simply commented, "If that were the case, we'd be sitting in these puddles for days. That'd be a whole lotta penalties." "That's kind of what I thought," she said. After we laughed so hard that we couldn't distinguish the tears from the rain, I told her about the hash marks.

Hash marks are the short lines on the field that mark every yard. (Notice in the following chart that the hash marks are set toward the middle of the field.) If a player with the ball goes out of bounds, the ball is **spotted** (marked) at that yard line, but it is placed on the closest hash mark. When the ball carrier is tackled anywhere between the hash marks and the sideline, the ball is placed on the closest hash mark. This is necessary so both the team with the ball and the opposing team have enough room to line up in a formation for the next play. The hash marks keep the plays close to the center of the field.

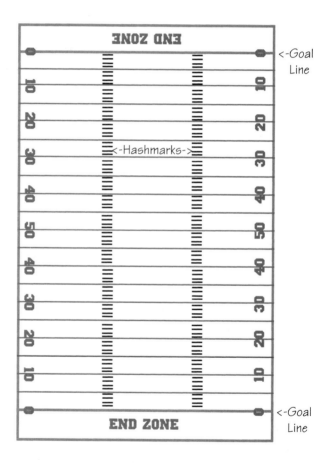

C. The Teams

Returning to my sister Kathryn's first football game, I remember the astonishment on her face when I said something about Stanford's different teams. She looked befuddled and then finally asked, "What? You mean there are more than two teams?" It sounds a little confusing, but the answer is yes and no. "Teams" can refer to the two sets of players from two different schools or cities, each with a team name, but within each of these teams, there are more teams or specialized groups of players. The different teams include offense, defense, and six "special teams." If you want to get technical, when you watch a football game, there are sixteen different units (teams) of players involved in the game. Hmmm . . . already you might be getting a sense that this game is a lot more complex than it appears on the surface! 'Tis true. But don't fret, here come the basics.

During the game, one team has eleven offensive players on the field, and the other team has eleven defensive players on the field. The rest of the players on both teams must stay off the field, behind the sidelines. If either team accidentally has more than eleven men on the field, they are penalized. In high school, some players play both offense and defense; in college and professional football, players usually play offense or defense, but not both.

Some players specialize throughout their football years and always play the same position. Others, however, learn to play various positions. Sometimes playing different positions is their choice; other times, they are assigned or moved to a different position by their coaches. Some position changes occur when players move from one level of play to another: middle school to high school, high school to college, or college to the pros. In high school, Kailee played running back (offense) and stayed on the field to play outside linebacker (defense). In college, he played defensive end. In the pros, he plays different linebacker positions.

Players have two sets of uniforms. One set of uniforms includes a colored jersey which represents the team's colors. The second set of uniforms has white jerseys. The colored jerseys represent the "home team," the team that is playing on its own field. Usually, players wearing the white jerseys are the visiting team. (You can also quickly tell the home team by the team logo and name printed on the field!) In addition to the colors of the uniforms, you can often identify players by the numbers that appear on their jerseys.

My sister once asked me why the sports announcers often commented about the number 13 on Kailee's Stanford jersey. I told her that a standard numbering system is usually used to identify players by their positions, but that Kailee's number was not consistent with the norm. Kailee wore number 3 throughout his high school varsity years. When he went to Stanford, number 3 was taken. When he was told he could choose another number, he chose "lucky 13," a number that is usually reserved for quarterbacks. He was a running back and a linebacker, but he was never a quarterback. Though a standard numbering system exists for all levels of football, many high school players are permitted to choose their own numbers, regardless of the standard numbering system. In college, many players are still given a choice, but the range of numbers is often restricted to the numbers within the standard numbering system. However, on occasion, you'll see players like Kailee, who do their own thing and for their own reasons choose a particular number to wear. Kailee now wears number 52, a number that is in the range reserved for linebackers.

The following chart shows the offensive and defensive players and their uniform numbers. If two sets of numbers are shown, the second set is used if the numbers in the first set are already taken by other players.

OFFENSIVE AND DEFENSIVE PLAYERS AND THEIR UNIFORM NUMBERS

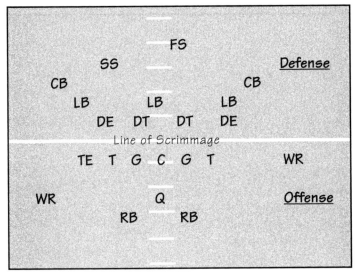

Defense

CB = cornerback (20-49)

DE = defensive end (60-79 or 90-99)

DT = defensive tackle (60-79 or 90-99)

FS = free safety (20-49)

LB = linebacker (50-59 or 90-99)

SS = strong safety (20-49)

Offense

C = center (50-59 or 60-69)

G = guard (60-79, 90-99)

Q = quarterback (1-19)

RB = running back (20-49)

T = tackle (60-79, 90-99)

TE = tight end (80-89)

WR = wide receiver (80-89 or 10-19)

There's so much to watch during a game! I don't think I'm different from most parents when I say I would often tape my son's games so I could go home and watch them again on TV. In addition to hearing the commentator's analyses and discussions, I could see things that I had missed during the game because my binoculars were focused on Kailee and not on the other parts of the field. If you have a person of "personal significance" on the field, you tend to watch him. If he's on the offensive team, you watch, cheer, and jump up and down for points to be scored. If your favored player is on defense, you hope to see powerful plays that stop the other team, shut them down, or push them back. It's difficult to watch all the action on the field. I learned a lot from watching the reruns, but I wonder what in the world I am going to do with the dozens upon dozens of tapes that are now stacked on shelves.

Offense

The offensive team on the field is the group of players who has the ball and strives to score points in the end zone. The quarterback (always an offensive player) can move the ball toward the end zone by:

1. handing or pitching the ball to a player who runs with the ball down the field,

2. passing (throwing) the ball to a player (a receiver) who catches the ball and runs with it,

   or

3. keeping the ball himself to try to pick up or move the ball forward a few more yards.

Score!

Each of the other ten offensive players is assigned to a specific position and has specific jobs on the field. The ultimate goal is always to be a part of a well-orchestrated plan to score points through touchdowns (six points), kicks for

extra points (PAT) after a touchdown, or **two-point con-versions,** which are also made after a touchdown in place of a PAT. When a touchdown seems unlikely, a field goal team may come onto the field to attempt a field goal (three points). You'll learn more about scoring points in Chapter 2.

Defense

Some of the terminology in football really is baffling when you think about it. Back to my dear sister. She asked, "What are they defending? The ball? Their half of the field? The goalpost? Themselves?" Hmmm, when you think about this, this really is a profound question! There are a lot of things (and body parts) to defend or protect out there on the field! But, simply put, they are defending their half of the field, which includes the red zone, the end zone, and their goal posts. In other words, they are protecting territory on their end of the field that, if invaded, could result in points for the other team.

The defensive team on the field tries to stop the offensive team from moving the ball forward and from scoring any points. Some of the defensive players focus on getting to the quarterback before he has the chance to pass the ball or hand the ball off to a running back. Three common terms relate specifically to plays where the defense goes after the quarterback:

1. **Sacking the quarterback**—The defense tackles the quarterback while he still has the ball and is still behind the line of scrimmage, the line where the play starts. When this happens, the offense loses yards on the play.

2. **Pass rushing**—When the quarterback drops back (steps back) to get ready to throw the ball, a defensive player storms toward the quarterback. The pass rusher tries to sack the quarterback, or at least put extra pressure on the quarterback and force him to pass prematurely or inaccurately.

3. **Blitzing**—Blitzing is an all-out attempt to get to the quarterback. An extra linebacker or defensive back is added to the defensive line to rush or put pressure on the quarterback. The ultimate goal is a **sack** (the quarterback is tackled with the ball behind the line of scrimmage).

Many times the quarterback can't be stopped, so the defensive team has to react to the action on the field. The defensive players try to force the offensive ball carrier to drop the ball (**fumble**) so the defense has a chance to recover and regain possession of the ball. The defensive players also watch for opportunities to catch (**intercept**) the ball when it is passed by the quarterback. When the defensive team gets the ball on a fumble or through an interception, the ball is **turned over** to the other team and the action moves in the other direction down the field. The battle goes on, back and forth, with the ball changing hands, and the action changing directions many times during the course of one game.

Tension is often high during football games, especially in stands packed with fans or during crucial games that determine playoff spots or championships. I shudder and cringe every time I think about one man whose son also played defense. Fortunately, he was not a "typical" parent. The father seldom yelled words of praise or encouragement. Instead, he yelled over and over at the top of his lungs, "Take no prisoners!" Now, that expression, mentality, and behavior to me were so inappropriate and brutal. I remember the number of times I wanted to stuff a sock in that boisterous mouth and tell him to calm down, and that it was "only a game." I went to great lengths to sit as far away from him as possible.

During Kailee's high school days, I almost always sat with my friend Debbie whose son Jimmy was also on the team. There was no doubt in anyone's mind that we were "parents." Somehow "parents" versus "interested fans" have a way of standing out!! We sat in the first few rows of the stadium so we could see everything . . . and be heard. It was all in good fun, and, besides, sometimes the cheerleaders needed a little extra help from the moms. Anyone who sat near us either joined in on the fun or were entertained by our festive antics. Many fond memories stem from the time shared with friends at football games!

D. The Line of Scrimmage

Lines, lines, lines. They're everywhere! Now with enhanced television, fans sitting at home can often see a yellow, computer-generated line on the field that shows how far the ball needs to be moved to make a first down. (I love that feature! It's too bad fans and players can't see it in the stadium and on the field.)

Even though the field has yard lines, hash marks, sidelines, and end lines, there is one invisible line that is mighty significant: the line of scrimmage. The line of scrimmage determines where players must line up at the beginning of a play, and it sets the basis for refs' penalty calls. You will notice in later chapters that many football rules relate to the line of scrimmage, so a basic understanding of this term is important. I guess there's some truth to one of my personal sayings, "There's power in what you can't see."

The **line of scrimmage** is an invisible line that passes through each end of the football when the football is placed on the field. The **neutral zone** is the distance between the two lines of scrimmage and is equal to the length of the football.

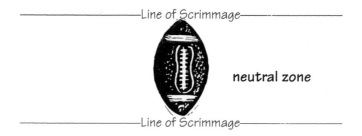

Some of the players on each team will line up on the line of scrimmage at the beginning of each play or each **down**. None of the offensive or defensive players on the line of scrimmage may move any part of his body, not even a finger, or have any part of his body over the line of scrimmage until the ball is snapped. The exception to this is the **center** (the offensive player who grips the ball and passes it between his legs to the quarterback), who is allowed to have his hand on the ball in the **neutral zone**.

If there is any movement, even very slight, by an offensive player on the line of scrimmage before the center snaps the ball, a **false start**, **offsides**, or **illegal shift** penalty is called. If an offensive player crosses over the line of scrimmage and moves into the neutral zone and makes contact with one of the defensive players, an **encroachment** penalty is called. If a false start, offsides, illegal shift, or encroachment is called on an offensive player, the offense will be penalized with a loss of yards: the

False start

ball will be placed five yards further *back* from the line of scrimmage for the next play. On the other hand, if a defensive player on the line of scrimmage moves into the neutral zone or moves offsides before the snap, or if he flinches even a little to make the offensive player come after him, a **neutral zone infraction** is called. With these defensive violations, the offense gets to move the ball *forward* five yards. These rules that penalize any type of movement on the line of scrimmage before the ball is put into play are enforced to prevent players on either team from getting a "head start," or a split second advantage over the other players.

Offsides

E. The Downs

Now, let's be logical. "Down" means down! I overheard a sweet, young woman who was sitting in front of me whisper into her boyfriend's ear, "Honey, you keep saying 'down.' Is that when the player goes down with the ball?" Well, I cannot adequately describe the look on his face after she whispered in his ear! His immediate response was, "Whaaat?" Poor thing. She was asking an innocent question about something she didn't quite understand. It's too bad more guys can't simply explain without turning a question into an embarrassing moment! I wanted to whisper to her, "It's an attempt to move the ball forward. They get four attempts or four 'downs' to go ten yards." However, I was caught back up in the game and didn't want to butt into their tender moments of snuggling and whispering. On second thought, I think the tender moments were only hers. His attention was on the game!

The offense, which is the team with the ball, has four chances to move the ball a total of ten yards toward the goal line. Each of these chances to move toward the opponent's end zone and score points is called a **down**. The scoreboard shows the down and the number of yards needed to complete the total of ten yards to get a new first down. For example, when you see "2nd down—5 yards," that means that the offensive team is on its second down (second attempt) and the offense has to move the ball five more yards in order to keep the ball and continue playing offense. If the offense does not move the ball all five yards on the second down, the team still has the third down and fourth down (attempts) to try to get the necessary yards.

First Down

If the ball carrier is tackled, the play is dead and so is one of the attempts. As soon as the ten yards is reached, the offense is given another **first down**, and has four new attempts to move the ball another ten yards. If they don't complete the ten yards and make another first down, they lose possession of the ball.

Sometimes the ball carrier is thrown for a loss or tackled for a loss. When this happens, the offense is pushed back and loses instead of gains yards. In other words, the ball carrier is tackled behind his own line of scrimmage. In the example above, the ball was "2nd and 5." If the ball carrier is tackled eight yards back behind the line of scrimmage, the offense would then be on the third down and have thirteen yards to go. If the offense can't move the ball forward the necessary thirteen yards in the third or the fourth down, they will lose possession of the ball. (Many times in this situation, they will **punt** the ball on the fourth down. See section G in this chapter.)

F. The Chains

A "chain gang" is used to help keep track of the yardage and the downs. The position of the chains is extremely important and affects the outcome of many games. I shudder when I remember my one experience on the chain gang. A man who always volunteered to move the chains simply did not show up for a flag football game which I was attending. One of the officials grabbed me (because I was sitting as close to the field as possible) and asked me to do the chains. I guess the official assumed I had been to enough games to know how to handle the chains. Unfortunately, this responsibility fell on me during my pre-enlightened years when I didn't know all that much about football. The official had no way of knowing that I never watched the actions of the members of the chain gang. Imagine how I felt after a few short plays when the ref stopped the game and yelled at me because I didn't move the chains correctly. I wanted to crawl in a hole and cry, but I didn't. Shortly after that, a father of one of the players showed up behind me and asked if I wanted to "be relieved of the duty." I said no and that I needed to redeem myself! However, I did ask him to hang around behind me and nudge me if I didn't move the chains when and where I was supposed to, or if it looked like I was going to move them when I shouldn't. Never, never, never again did I find myself down near the sidelines at the beginning of a game before the chain gang members were stationed on the field. Once was enough.

The chains on the sidelines mark the ten yards that need to be covered in four attempts or four downs. As soon as the ball has been successfully moved ten yards, the chains are moved to show the next ten yards needed to keep pos-

session of the ball. One of the interesting and important statistics for a game is the number of first downs a team is able
to make during a game. You want your team to get as many
first downs as possible!

G. The Fourth Down

"Why the !*?# didn't they go for it? Why didn't they kick it? Who made that stupid call?" In any football crowd, everyone has an opinion and everyone seems to become an "expert." Of course, if you are watching on TV, you have the sports announcers to contend with, and they all have their own authoritative opinions. The range of comments from all these "experts" cracks me up. Fourth downs often become moments of intense drama: it's decision-making time, and the coaches are either praised or criticized for their fourth down decisions. The team is either going to make a great play to gain the necessary yardage for a new first down, or the ball is going to be turned over to the other team. An offense is having a heck of a great day if they have a lot of first downs and don't end up with many fourth downs. After reading the section below, you'll be better equipped to appreciate the drama that unfolds the next time your team is faced with a fourth down.

Fourth Down

On the **fourth down,** the position on the field often determines the next play that will be called. The offense does not want to give the opponent good field position if it has to turn the ball over to them. On the fourth down, again depending on the field position, there are three options that can be exercised:

1. *Go for it!* If the offense is working well, if there is only a yard or two needed, or if the team with the ball is close to the goal line, one more play may be called with the hopes of either making another first down or scoring. For short yardage, one player may attempt to carry the ball to make enough yardage for a new first down. The ball carrier will likely face a brick wall of defensive players assembled to prevent him from

making the short yardage. On occasion, the quarterback decides to keep the ball and attempts to plow through the defensive players to gain the necessary yards. This play is called the **quarterback sneak**. If the offense is close to the end zone, the quarterback may also opt to throw the ball to a player for additional yards or a touchdown. None of these plays, however, is generally used if the team is too far up field (too far away from the goal line to score and too close to the other team's goal line), because the risk is too great. If the offense fails to make a few yards needed for a new first down, the other team will be given a field advantage by having the ball closer to their scoring end zone.

2. *Kick a field goal!* If the offense is close enough to the end zone, usually around the 30-yard line, the **field goal kicking team** may come onto the field for the fourth down to attempt to kick the ball through the goal posts. If the ball goes through the goal posts, or the uprights, the team scores three points for a **field goal**. (Field goals will be discussed in Chapters 2 and 5.)

3. *Punt the ball away!* When the offense needs too many yards to make a first down or is too far away from the end zone to attempt a field goal, a special team called the **punting team** comes in to **punt** (kick) the ball as far downfield as possible. The defense will send in a **punt return team** to receive the ball. (The punting teams are discussed in Chapter 5.)

H. The Length of the Game

The clock never tells the whole story! The length of the game is determined by the number of penalties, the number of time-outs, and whether or not the game is televised. (Moms of young ones: the time-outs are not the kind you give your kids. Time-outs do not occur when the players are "misbehaving." On second thought, sometimes time-outs are given when the players seem disorganized and need to settle down. Maybe there is a similarity!) Commercial breaks, needless to say, lengthen the time of the game.

From the fans' point of view, the length of the game is also determined by the weather and the performance of the team. Some games seem mighty long when the wind is blowing, the rain is pelting down, the damp fog sets in, or the team is dismally losing the game. The Viking–Packer game in Green Bay in 1998 was perhaps one of the longest games I ever endured. I cannot even begin to tell you how much it rained, how little my rain gear did its job, how wet I was right to the skin, and how frustrating it was to have the rain ruin my binoculars. I was so miserable that I didn't even see Kailee make an interception. (Ah, but then there was the video version waiting for me at home!) The opposite occurred at the Denver game in 1999. I packed enough heavy clothes to withstand a blizzard. Just in case the weather forecasters were wrong, on an impulse, I also packed a pair of shorts. The Denver game was uncomfortably long for many fans who wore heavy clothes—jeans, sweaters, gloves, and hats. They were caught off guard by the eighty-degree day—but they at least were able to remove their gloves and hats.

A regular football game, without any overtime (used in tie games) consists of **four quarters** that are each fifteen minutes long (twelve minutes in high school football). The actual length of the game, however, lasts more than one hour due to **time-outs** that may be called by the teams, by the officials, or by television broadcasters for commercials. Each team is allowed to call three time-outs during each half of the game; time-outs are used to discuss or change the game plan, to talk to the coaches, or to get better organized.

Time-out

At the end of a time-out, the referee places the ball on the **line of scrimmage**. The quarterback then has forty seconds to get the play started. A time clock is shown on the field. If the quarterback does not start in time, a **delay of game** penalty is called. The team is given a five-yard penalty and has to move back five yards and **repeat the down** (start over but start the action five yards back from the previous line of scrimmage). This rule helps move the game along and prevents teams from controlling the length of a game.

Delay of Game

In addition to the time-outs, the clock stops for a variety of reasons throughout the game, such as scoring, penalties, injuries, punts, fair catches, turnovers, and players running out of bounds. Between the second and the third quarter, there is also **halftime**, a short break in which players retreat to the locker rooms and fans can take their own breaks!

Making good use of the halftime break requires some strategies. Many people forego halftime entertainment and take the opportunity to visit the restroom. Women, beware! Rarely will you see long lines form outside men's restrooms, but the women's lines can go halfway around the stadium! If you must make the visit, don't dally or, guaranteed, you'll miss part of the second half. It's often impossible to visit the restroom and make your way to the front of the line at the refreshment

stand before the kick off gets underway on the field. Fortunately, women are resourceful and will find ways to deal with
these dilemmas.

As you watch and listen to games, you will become
aware of the many references to the clock. Some plays, especially toward the ends of the first and second halves of
the game, are designed to "keep the clock running" while
other plays are designed to "stop the clock," whichever is
most advantageous to the team in possession of the ball. A
few seconds at the end of the game can make a difference
and determine the winner.

Just a few seconds of game time have proven decisive time and
time again. By December 22, 1999, fifteen games of the 1999
NFL season were won in the final ten seconds. (Knowing this, I
simply cannot comprehend how fans could pay good money to
attend a game and then leave before it's over. Yet, you'll see
throngs of fans leave in the last five or ten minutes to avoid
the post-game traffic! Truly now, does that make any sense?)
Following are a few other interesting statistics. An average
quarterback snap is three-tenths of a second. A quarterback
drops back for a pass in 2 to 3 seconds. An average play lasts
5 to 6 seconds. The air time for a kick off ball is 4.2 to 4.3
seconds, and the air time for a punt is 4.5 seconds. Needless
to say, a few seconds can make a difference in the outcome of
a game.[1]

When only two minutes remain in the first half and the
end of the game, a **two-minute warning** is given by the
referees. Teams often seem to play at an accelerated (and
more aggressive) pace; a **hurry-up offense** may be used in
which the quarterback throws a lot of passes and the re-

---

1   "Scott Bosck and the Elias Sports Bureau for the Minnesota
    Vikings," *USA Today*, December 22, 1999.

ceivers try to catch the ball and run out-of-bounds to stop the clock. The goal is to move the ball as quickly as possible with hopes of scoring before the end of the half or the end of the game.

When I was once yelling "hurry up and score," at the TV screen (as though the players could really hear me), one of my friends asked me about the thing called "hurry-up offense." "Why," she pondered out loud, "don't they use that hurry up thing throughout the game?" I explained that the hurry-up offense involves a lot of passes and the use of the hurry-up offense increases the risk of interceptions; in no more than a split second, the team can lose possession of the ball. If hurry-up offense were to be used too often, the play would become predictable to the opponent and the likelihood of interceptions would increase. Besides, disciplined use of the hurry-up offense transforms those last two minutes into a special kind of dramatic air show performed under fire and fueled by guts and determination. Who would want to miss that sudden burst of desperate energy and the nail-biting excitement? Not me.

I. The Kick Off

For many people, the coin toss that precedes the beginning of a game (the kick off) signals the beginning of the game. For others, the beginning of the game begins with their pregame rituals which include elaborate tailgate parties. For me, my pregame ritual is quiet, serious, and private. I pray. I pray for the safety of all players. I pray for a game with no injuries. I have a special prayer for Kailee that is always the same. Kailee, like most players, has his own set of pregame rituals that begin well before he is taped and in his uniform. In high school, it was essential for him to eat my lasagna before a game. When there were early games, I raced home from my job with just enough time to assemble the "lucky meal." In college, his ritual was to have turkey, mashed potatoes, and vanilla ice cream the night before the game, and chicken and spaghetti right before the game. Now his ritual is based less on food and more on his choice of activities. He prefers spending most of his pregame or travel time in quiet settings by himself, away from crowds and distractions. He always listens to one favorite CD that gets him in his "mindset." Why do people adopt such rituals? Perhaps it's because the specific behaviors provide a familiar and comforting structure, or perhaps it's simply because they are associated with the desired results.

At the beginning of the game, a coin is tossed. A captain from each team is involved in the coin toss. The winner of the coin toss has four options: start the game by kicking the ball to the other team, start the game by receiving the ball, select a specific goal to defend, or defer the choice to the beginning of the second half. In the NFL, usually the winner of the coin toss chooses to receive the kick off and begin the game as offense and, hopefully, score the first points of the game. In high school and college, the winner of the coin toss often chooses to defer the choice to the beginning of the second half. However, other considerations may be involved in making the decision, such as wanting to defend a specific half of the field because of wind or weather factors.

"The anthem is over. What's everybody doing?" My friend, the non-football friend, was ready to sit down after we'd sung "America the Beautiful." That's a no-no. You just have to be a part of the escalating excitement of a kick off! The kick-off team is positioned in a line that stretches across most of the field. When the ball is kicked, the players run fast, I mean really fast, down the field in that impressive and intimidating straight line formation. They head directly into the opposing team. The action is swift. Players fly all over the place, and from the onslaught of determined players, a player with the ball may emerge, break through the tackles and head further downfield. Ohhhh . . . kick offs send chills up my spine (and sometimes even tears to my eyes). Kick offs truly are to be enjoyed standing up!

A **kick off** is the first play of the game following the coin toss and the first play in the second half of the game (the third quarter). A kick off also occurs after a team scores a touchdown and attempts the point after a touchdown and after a field goal is kicked. For kick off, the ball is placed on the 30-yard line (or the 35-yard line in college or the 40-yard line in high school). The **place kicker** places the ball on a tee. When the referee blows the whistle to begin the game, the place kicker kicks the ball as far as possible down the field to the kick-off return team. (Kick off teams are discussed in Chapter 5.)

I don't know about you, but with my wildest imagination, I simply cannot imagine being hit head-on or pulled to the ground by a herd of powerful, muscular men in tight pants and massive shoulder pads! The kick returner, the player who catches and runs with the kick off ball, faces such a herd several times in every game. Incomprehensible! Without a doubt, this position requires some serious mental fortitude. I've always thought it would be interesting to embed a small camera in the helmet of a kick returner so we could get a sense of what it is like to have a hungry pack of players charging straight at us with only one thought in mind.

On the kick off, one of the following events usually occurs:

1. The receiver (the kick returner) catches the ball and runs as far as possible toward the goal line, where the points are scored. Sometimes the kick returner is able to run the entire length of the field and score a touchdown on a kick off. The play, however, usually ends when the ball carrier is tackled, runs out of bounds, or fumbles (drops or loses) the ball. When the player is tackled or runs out of bounds, the ball is **dead**. The ball is then placed on the closest hash mark and the yard line where the play was ruled as over. The first down begins from that location on the field.

   A **fumble** occurs when the ball carrier loses his hold on the ball or the ball is **stripped** out of his hands by a defensive player. For a fumble to be called, the player must lose control of the ball *before* one of his knees hits the ground. If the player loses his grip on the ball *after* his knee hits the ground, there is no fumble because the ball is considered dead and the play is over as soon as his knee hits the ground. If the ball is fumbled, the team that ends up with the ball recovers it and the next play begins at the place where

Dead Ball   the ball was recovered.

2. The ball is kicked **out of bounds**. The kicking team is penalized and the ball is re-kicked from five yards farther back from where they started.

During a crucial play in a play-off game, a young boy asked his dad, "Was that a fumble?" His dad replied, " I don't know." "Why, Daddy? Why don't you know? The guy fell down." That must have been tough for a dad to admit that he didn't know! Sometimes even the officials aren't sure if there was a fumble. The decision is based on whether or not the player had control of the ball at the split second that his knee hit the ground.

In the NFL, a good number of plays undergo the scrutiny of an instant replay to determine whether or not the ball was fumbled. College and high school games don't allow the instant replay, so the referees do not have the opportunity to get a second look. They must simply use their best judgment to make the call when the play happens on the field. Since the action on the field occurs so quickly, sometimes the referees' calls are correct, and other times they are major blunders.

J. The Action Continues

As soon as the official starts the clock, the offensive team has forty seconds to get the play started. Some of the offensive players and some of the defensive players line up on the line of scrimmage.

One offensive player, the center, positions himself on the line of scrimmage, grips the ball on the ground, and snaps the ball by passing it between his legs to the quarterback. Until the ball is snapped, all the players on both lines of scrimmage must remain stationary; no player on the line of scrimmage can move a single part of his body or move into the neutral zone. (Remember that a five-yard penalty is the consequence of a false start/offsides, encroachment, or neutral zone infraction before the ball is snapped.) Only one offensive player behind the line of scrimmage may be moving **(man in motion).**

Once the ball is snapped, the players on both teams make their moves, quickly and forcefully. The offense tries to outsmart, out-move, and out-block the defense in order to pick up yards, move the ball forward, and eventually score points. Of course, the defense is putting forth all its effort to stop the ball from moving forward and to protect its end of the field.

The defense tries to disrupt the play or stop the ball carrier as soon as possible to prevent him from gaining yards. Once the ball is **dead**, meaning the ball carrier is stopped or the play is disrupted, a new down begins. Remember, the offense has four downs (attempts) to move the ball ten yards. As soon as ten yards is reached, a new **first down** begins.

2
SCORING POINTS

Have you ever entered a Super Bowl pool with coworkers or friends? In many football pools, you draw or select a number and if the winning team scores the number of points reflected by the number you have, you win the pool of money. For one pool, a friend ended up with a twenty-five. "How in the world am I supposed to win with this number?" she asked. "They can score six or they can score three. I know my math well enough to know that those combinations don't add up to twenty-five." Well, she may know her math, but she doesn't know the point system for football! Actually, there are several combinations of points that could make twenty-five. It's not the greatest number to have, but it can be reached with combinations of one, two, three, and six points.

Compared to so many other aspects of football which have a way of quickly becoming complex, scoring is relatively easy to understand. Every team has only five ways to score points. The most highly sought-after points are those made by touchdowns. Getting a touchdown is rewarded with an opportunity to make one or two additional points. If a touchdown is not within reach, the next best option is a field goal. Touchdowns, extra points after a touchdown, and field goals are the pride of the offense; they work hard to get those points on the board. The fifth way to score is quite the reverse of the other four methods: when you read about the safety, you'll see who did the work to earn those points!

The following chart summarizes the five ways to score points in football.

Touchdown	6 points
Point After	1 point
Two-Point Conversion	2 points
Field Goal	3 points
Safety	2 points

A. Touchdown – Six points

A **touchdown** is made when the offensive player gets into the end zone with the ball to score. A ball carrier may run across the goal line or "make it into the end zone." The ball carrier may be tripped or tackled before he reaches the end zone, but a touchdown is still scored if he gets the ball to "break the plane" of the end zone line before he actually hits the ground. In other words, if the ball makes it over the end zone line but the player's entire body doesn't, a touchdown is still scored.

A touchdown may also be scored on a pass. An offensive player (usually the **receiver**) catches a pass and then runs the ball into the end zone. Or, the receiver may be inside the end zone waiting for the ball to be sent his way. As soon as he catches the ball and shows he has control of the ball, a touchdown is scored. When a receiver catches the ball in the end zone, the position of his feet is very important. In high school, one foot must be inside the end zone at the time the ball is caught or the play is not counted as a touchdown. In college and the pros, *both* feet must be inside the end zone when the ball is caught or a touchdown is not scored. In all levels of football, the player cannot be juggling or bobbling the ball; he must have visible control or a definite hold on the ball. This judgment is made by the referees. As you will often notice during touchdowns, a fine-tuned sense of timing and body positioning make the difference between a touchdown or no score at all.

Score!

B. Point After – One point

The announcer during one game said, "Well, here comes P-A-T." My friend laughed and said, "That's really stupid. Why didn't he just say the player's name instead of spelling it?" Well, dear friend, there is no "Pat." It's not the name of the coach, the name of the kicker, or the name of any other player. Every team is going to have a P-A-T, which is an acronym for "point after touchdown." Here's what the P-A-T is all about!

After a touchdown, the offense sends in its special kicking team (**PAT team**) to attempt to score one more point by kicking the ball through the uprights and over the crossbar of the goal posts. The center snaps the ball to a player who holds the ball for the **place kicker**. The place kicker takes a few steps and gives the ball one quick boot toward the goal posts. If the ball is kicked through the goal posts, one point is scored. The PAT teams are discussed further in Chapter 5.

C. Two-Point Conversion –
Two points

"Oh, noooo! They're going for it! They're going for it! I can't believe they're going for it! Oh no, they'll never make it. Oh, why are they going for it? Wow! They did it! They did it! Man, I knew they could do it! Wow! What a play!"

Conversations such as the one above often sound confusing and contradictory, but a little explanation will clarify the concerns expressed in the above conversation. Instead of attempting the extra point by kicking, the team opts to attempt a more difficult two-point conversion play. One minute the fans yell for the team to try for the two-point play, but then fearing the team won't make the play and will lose the opportunity for an extra point, they yell for a one-point play instead. The emotions go up and down in anticipation of the play and up and down afterwards when the outcome is known!

After a touchdown, the offense may attempt to carry the ball across the goal line or pass the ball to a player who is in the end zone instead of kicking for the extra PAT. This play, called **two-point conversion**, is much riskier and much more difficult to complete. The ball is snapped to the quarterback who then either hands the ball to another player, passes the ball to a receiver, or sometimes tries to run the ball over the goal line himself. If the offense gets the ball across the goal line, it scores two points. The two-point conversion is usually more difficult to make than the one point made by the kicker, but players, coaches, and fans know that one extra point often determines the winner of a close game. On rare occasions, the ball may be intercepted or fumbled. In high school, the ball is then ruled dead. In college and the NFL, the other team can attempt to run the ball down the entire field to score two points. The two-point conversion play is discussed more in Chapter 5.

D. Field Goal – Three points

When the offense is on the fourth down and close to the goal line (usually within thirty yards), a decision may be made to attempt a **field goal** for three points. The ball is snapped to a player who holds the ball for the **field goal** kicker. If the field goal is good, the offense scores three points. The ball is then placed on the 30-yard line (just like a kick off) and turned over to the other team.

If the field goal attempt is no good, the other team takes over on the yard line where the ball was kicked. (In high school, the ball is placed on the 20-yard line.) Because the other team gains possession at the point of the attempt, many times a field goal attempt from too far away is not the best option for a play. The opponent would gain an excellent field position or advantage if the field goal is missed. In such a situation, the ball usually is punted away (see Chapter 5) instead of kicked for a field goal attempt. A field goal attempt may also be made in the last few seconds of a half or the end of the game when there is time for one final play.

E. Safety – Two points

When you hear the word "safety," what do you think of? Do you think of feeling secure and out of harm's way? Well, that's logical. In the world of football, the term "safety" can take on two very different meanings. In Chapter 4, you will learn that "safety" is the name of a position for a defensive back who is in the backfield and farthest from the line of scrimmage. Terming his position as a "safety" makes sense. He tries to keep the backfield "safe." When the term is used in scoring, it refers to a situation that occurs when the ball carrier, to his embarrassment, frustration, and dismay, is caught in the wrong place with the ball. He actually scores points for the other team! Now, for a competitive man and otherwise skilled player, that's a hard knock to the ego. Why does "safety" have two completely different meanings? Maybe it's designed to keep us mentally sharp.

A **safety** (two points) is scored when a defensive player tackles an offensive player with the ball inside the wrong end zone. The offense struggles to make a play to move the ball toward the other end of the field where they can score, but the quarterback or the ball carrier can't get rid of the ball or can't get out of the end zone with the ball in time. This unusual situation tends to occur when the quarterback or the ball carrier either steps or is forced by the defense into the wrong end zone. *Bang!* A defensive player tackles him with the ball in the wrong end zone and scores two points! The error made by the ball carrier actually puts points on the score board for the opposing team. Needless to say, offensive teams try not to be caught in this embarrassing situation.

Safety

3
OFFENSIVE PLAYERS

OK, I agree, there are a lot of players and a lot of positions. If you have a son, boyfriend, or friend playing football, it's important to know the name of his position and what the position entails. Standing on the sidelines at one game, I met a mother whose son was just starting out on the team. I casually asked, "What position does your son play?" Expecting a simple answer, I was flabbergasted when she responded, "Well, I must admit I don't really know very much about football. I don't know what position he plays, but I know he bends over." Well, I thought to myself, ask no more. At least I knew he wasn't the kicker.

A. Basic Offensive Formation

Twenty-two players are on the field for every play. Eleven players belong to the offense and eleven to the defense. If special teams are on the field, there will still be only twenty-two players on the field. Realize, however, that teams have much bigger rosters so they have extra players to send in (to substitute) for the starters in the various positions. Terms such as "backup quarterback" or "second in line" refer to players who are sent in to play when the starting player is taken out of the game.

As mentioned in Chapter 1, the term offense is used for the team that has the ball and the team that will try to score points. The offense consists of eleven players. Seven of the offensive players must line up on the line of scrimmage at the beginning of each play. (An **illegal formation** penalty is called if there are not seven players on the line of scrimmage.) One common offensive formation, or lineup of players, is shown below.

Illegal
Formation

Basic Offense Chart

Line of Scrimmage

TE T G C G T   WR

WR   Q

RB   RB

C = center   T = tackle
G = guard   TE = tight end
Q = quarterback   WR = wide receiver
RB = running back

This formation uses one quarterback, five offensive line-men, one tight end, two wide receivers, and two running backs. However, for different offense formations, the running backs, tight end, and wide receivers may be positioned in different parts of the field, or they may use different combinations of players (such as four receivers, one running back, and no tight end, or three receivers, one running back, and one tight end).

Now, all this may sound confusing. Fortunately, some of the names for player positions reveal something about the nature of the position. As Kailee once said, as he jogged in a pool while I was trying to nail down his ideas for this section, "Just think about it. If you are on the line, you are a 'lineman.' If you are the 'center,' you are in the center of the line. If you are a 'linebacker' [also referred to as "back" or "backer"], you are back behind the line. If you are a 'running back,' you run. If you are a 'receiver,' you receive or catch." Then he dove under the water, and I was left to ponder some of the other names for offensive positions that aren't quite as logical. (I think he dove to the bottom to avoid these questions.) How can a player have a "full back," "half a back," a "quarter of a back," or the "back of a tail?" Then, my own light bulb went on. All of these terms reflect distances from the line of scrimmage. The quarterback is a quarter of the way behind the line of scrimmage. The halfback is half the way back, and, logically speaking, the fullback is the full or whole way in back of the line of scrimmage. A "flanker" is on the flank or the side of the field. (Think of a flank of beef; it's the same idea!) That left me pondering, " How can a player have "a split end" or a "tight end?" (Oops, don't answer that one.)

Five of the offensive players are called **linemen** because they are lined up right on the line of scrimmage. The linemen include one **center**, two **guards**, and two **tackles**. The center is in the center of the lineup. The two guards are placed to the right and to the left of the center. The tackles line up next to the guards. These five linemen are *ineligible* to catch a pass. The remaining two offensive players on the line of scrimmage are called *eligible receivers* because they are eligible to catch a pass and are postitioned one on each end. The offense uses many different offensive formations, so the way players line up on the line of scrimmage at the beginning of a play will vary. In a basic offensive formation, a **tight end** and a **wide receiver** will be on the line of scrimmage. The tight end will be on one end of the line up (or formation) and the wide receiver will be on the opposite end of the formation. A second wide receiver will be behind the line of scrimmage. The **quarterback**, who is the "field general" of the team, lines up behind the center. The center will snap the ball to the quarterback to begin the play.

The two remaining players that make up the eleven man offense are the **running backs**. The running backs may also be called fullbacks, halfbacks, or tailbacks, depending on the type of formation that is used. These two players as well as the tight ends and the wide receivers are eligible to receive the ball.

B. The Quarterback

As previously mentioned, the quarterback is the "field general" of the offense. The quarterback has the job of calling the offensive plays in the **huddle**. When you see the players in a tight-knit circle on the field, bending over and listening to the quarterback's directions for the next play, the team is in the huddle.

In high school and college football, the coaching staff's offensive coordinator usually determines which play to call. The quarterback looks toward the sidelines to get a hand signal that is a secret code for the play to call. Usually, several different coaches send signals from the sidelines, but only one coach signals the actual play that the quarterback will use. The other coaches are simply decoys to confuse the opponent and prevent the opponent from getting an edge by knowing the play in advance.

In the pros, the calling of plays is more sophisticated. The quarterback has speakers inside his helmet. The offensive coordinator can speak directly to the quarterback when the quarterback has his men gathered around him in the

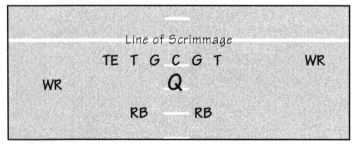

C = center   T = tackle
G = guard   TE = tight end
Q = quarterback   WR = wide receiver
RB = running back

huddle. Plays are sent into the huddle through the helmet rather than hand signals from the sidelines.

Because the offense wants to keep its intended play a secret from the opponent, it uses a secret **snap count** to surprise the defense with the timing of the start of the play. In the huddle, the quarterback also tells his players the snap count. The snap count tells the players when the center will put the ball into play, that is, when he will "snap" the ball to the quarterback. When the offense goes to the line of scrimmage, it is important that every offensive player knows the snap count. If a player on the line of scrimmage moves too soon before the ball is snapped, the team is penalized; if the player moves too late, he will have his opponent "in his face." Snap counts vary from play to play and from team to team. For example, for one play, the snap count might be the first sound made by the quarterback. As soon as he opens his mouth, the ball is snapped. Other times the snap count will involve a series of numbers and colors. The quarterback may say something like, "on two, down, set, blue forty-six, blue forty-six, blue forty-six, go, go, go." The "blue forty-six" is a secret code for a specific play. The ball would be snapped on the second "go." It's easy to see how players can get confused, take off too soon, or hesitate too long on the line of scrimmage!

> "The best thing about playing quarterback in the NFL is the challenge of being the on-the-field leader and competing on the highest level of football in the world."
>
> —Quarterback Daunte Culpepper, Minnesota Vikings

Sometimes the quarterback gets up to the line of scrimmage and sees that the play he intended to call won't work with the defensive formation that is lined up and ready to attack. In such a situation, the quarterback may call an **audible**. An audible is a call that is made at the line of scrimmage in order to adjust to the defensive formation on the field. The audible is not the play that was called in the huddle. Sharp, alert players need to be ready to adjust mentally and physically to the abrupt change of plans.

In my "earlier years," I found myself frequently asking Kailee for clarification. I knew there was a lot that I didn't understand. "Kailee, can anyone catch the ball thrown by the quarterback?" "No, Mom. Only the running backs, the tight ends, and the wide receivers are eligible to catch the ball." Now I know what he really meant: the running backs (which can also be fullbacks, halfbacks, tailbacks, and even split backs) and the wide receivers (which can be split ends or flankers) and the tight ends (which are receivers) can catch the ball. Now it's much clearer, right?

The quarterback gets into position behind the center and gives the snap count. The center snaps the ball into the hands of the quarterback. The quarterback hands the ball to a running back for a running play or passes the ball to a wide receiver, a tight end, or a running back for a passing play. (Remember that tackles, guards, and the center, known as the offensive linemen, are ineligible to receive the ball.) The quarterback may also keep the ball himself (**a quarterback sneak**) to try to make a short yardage play to get a first down. After a game has been played and analyzed, the stats (statistics) for the game will show the number of yards gained by passing the ball (**passing yards**), the percentage of passes completed, the number of yards gained by handing the ball to a runner (**rushing yards**), and the number of interceptions, fumbles, and sacks.

When the quarterback throws the ball, he cannot go past the line of scrimmage. He must throw the ball from *behind* the line of scrimmage. The quarterback tries to stay in the pocket long enough for a wide receiver, tight end, or running back to get to a place on the field free from the defensive players and open (available) to receive the ball. The

pocket is an area formed around the quarterback by his team's offensive linemen who try to block the incoming defensive players and protect the quarterback long enough for him to throw a pass. You will see the quarterback **drop back** (take a few steps back) in the pocket to time his pass to the receiver, but he tries to stay inside the pocket at all times. If the quarterback moves outside of the pocket, he was likely forced out by the incoming defensive players; his chances of getting sacked or tackled are increased. The quarterback **scrambles** when he has to run with the ball himself because no receiver is open to catch a pass. When the quarterback scrambles, he runs to get as many yards as possible and may end the play by sliding with his feet forward. The quarterback cannot be hit when he is sliding to end the play.

Fans go wild at the sight of a sack! The quarterback's fans shake their heads in disbelief (and disgust), moan, groan, and indulge in a variety of negative gestures and utterances. The fans of the defensive team shout with sheer joy and know how great that sack felt to the defensive player who "got in there" and "got to the quarterback" behind the line of scrimmage. You should see what happens to moms when a sack is delivered by their sons. Everyone knows a sack is a big deal and a cause for a celebration.

A **sack** occurs when one or more defensive players break through the offensive line and tackle the quarterback while he still has the ball behind the line of scrimmage. If the quarterback is tackled past the line of scrimmage, it is considered a tackle, not a sack. An **interception** occurs when the quarterback throws a pass but instead of one of his players catching the ball, a player on the defensive team catches the ball. In the case of an interception, the ball is turned over; the other team gains possession of the ball. An **intentional grounding** occurs when the quarterback is in

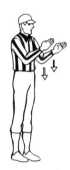

Intentional
Grounding

the pocket and throws the ball to an area that has no player in the vicinity to receive the ball. An intentional grounding is sometimes done to avoid getting sacked; the result is usually a ten-yard penalty and a loss of that down. In specific situations, however, only a loss of the down may occur.

Because the quarterback has such a key role on the team, extra protection is given to him. Defensive players may rush through the offensive line and tackle or sack the quarterback before he releases the ball. If a defensive player makes contact with the quarterback after he releases the ball, there is a fifteen-yard **roughing the passer** penalty against the defensive player and the offense gets an automatic first down.

Personal Foul
Roughing
the Passer

Led by the quarterback, the offense uses different strategies to outguess or outwit the other team by predicting their game plan and adjusting accordingly. The defense does the same. The many offensive and defensive strategies involved quickly become complex, and, quite honestly, involve more than the novice fan needs to know, so this discussion will focus on the basics. In addition to the terms already discussed, the following terms are often used to discuss the activity of the quarterback:

1. **The bomb**—As you might guess, a bomb is an extremely long pass. The quarterback wants to make a big play, so he gets deep in the pocket and gives his throw all he's got. If a bomb is completed, the offense finds itself much farther downfield and closer to scoring, or it scores a touchdown.

2. **Hail Mary**—A Hail Mary is another long pass play. It is an "all or nothing" play that is the quarterback's last desperate attempt to score. A Hail Mary usually happens at the end of the first half or at the end of the game and is thrown by the team that is behind in the scoring.

3. **Play-Action-Pass**—The quarterback tries to confuse or trick the defense by faking a handoff to a running back. The defense runs in to cover the play, but the quarterback then drops back to pass. The defense loses some momentum as it realizes the ball will be passed and has to move back in the field to defend against a pass play.

4. **Shotgun**—Shotgun is a special type of offense that is used for a long pass. Normally, the quarterback stays in the pocket and either hands the ball to a running back, or he drops back, which means he takes a few steps back, and looks for a receiver who is open to receive a pass. The defense often does not know with certainty whether the play will be a running play or a passing play. They wait for some type of indicator from the quarterback. However, with the shotgun, the defense knows that the quarterback is going for a long pass play because the quarterback begins the play by standing farther back in the pocket. By starting farther back from the line of scrimmage, the receivers will have more time to run down the field, and the quarterback (hopefully) will have more time to get the ball into the air and into an available receiver's hands.

5. **Quarterback Option**—The quarterback tries to run around the end of the defensive line and then up the field. The quarterback also has the option (depending what is happening on the field) to throw a lateral (sideways) pass to a running back. This offensive play is used in high school and college football, but seldom in the NFL.

6. **Pump Fake**—The quarterback acts as though he is going to throw the ball in a specific direction to a receiver. However, he holds on to the ball and then throws the ball to a different receiver who is in a different area of the field. The quarterback hopes to trick the defense by getting them to run to a part of the field where he will not be throwing the ball.

All these plays may sound a bit confusing at first, but these do make sense. A bomb is a bomb; it hits the target. A Hail Mary, without being sacrilegious, is a "blessed bomb" based on a desperate hope and faith. For a play-action-pass, the play begins, then there's new action, and then there's a pass. For the shotgun, the quarterback steps back to get ready to "shoot" the ball down the field. The pump fake speaks for itself.

Bombs and Hail Marys can take your breath away! Players, coaches, and fans hold their breaths in suspended silence that finally ends with ecstatic cheers or sorrowful moans. I am amused by people who can remember exact plays, who did what, the time left on the clock, and even which teams were playing. I don't have a mind prone to trivia, but I know that I have been delirious with joy on more than one occasion when "the thing of beauty" occurred "for my team."

C. The Center

Watch the center carefully and this question may cross your mind. "Doesn't the center feel weird having someone's hands right there like that between his legs and on his behind?" Now, there's a question you probably wouldn't feel comfortable asking a center. My simple response is, "I'm sure he's used to it by now!" This somewhat intimate route is used to get the ball to the quarterback.

The center stands at the center of the offense's line of scrimmage and is the central figure in the play. His job is to listen to the quarterback and to snap the ball to the quarterback on the right snap count. He also tries to "read the defense" and give directions or assignments to the other linemen. A fumble can occur if the center has a bad

> "I like playing center because the center is the central nervous system of the offense. It is the most cerebral of all the positions. The center makes all the line calls and adjustments, not to mention that the play can't start until I snap the ball."
>
> -Center Matt Birk, Minnesota Vikings

Line of Scrimmage

TE T G **C** G T   WR

WR   Q

RB   RB

C = center
G = guard
Q = quarterback
RB = running back

T = tackle
TE = tight end
WR = wide receiver

snap and the ball doesn't get into the quarterback's hands.
The center's job after the snap is to block incoming defensive players who hope to disrupt the offensive play. The
center may also be the snapper on one of the special teams,
in which case he snaps the ball to a punter or to a player
who holds the ball for the kicker to kick. Special teams are
discussed in Chapter 5.

D. Two Guards and Two Tackles

At the beginning of games, I often look at the size of the lineup for the opposing team. On a few occasions, my eyes almost pop out of my head at the sight of some of the *huge* players! I begin to pray, literally, for the well-being of any defensive player whose horrendous task is to contain a 300- to 360-pound guard or tackle. The body size of many offensive players on the line of scrimmage definitely makes an intimidating statement! Don't be misled by a little belly hanging over the pants. The *big* guys are very capable of creating havoc on the field and are often the concrete barriers that frustrate defenses and put fear in the hearts of moms who watch their moves closely through binoculars. If the numbers on their jerseys are 60–79 or 90–99, you're getting an eye full of a guard or a tackle.

I remember asking Kailee once what goes through his head when he is matched up with a player who outweighs him by a hundred pounds. He told me how he and other players focus on their own speed and quickness which they use to their advantage to get around these massive barriers. What looks like a mismatch in size may actually be a mismatch in speed and agility.

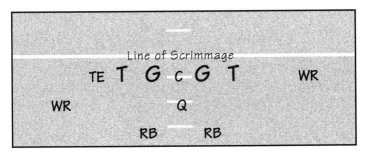

C = center
G = guard
Q = quarterback
RB = running back

T = tackle
TE = tight end
WR = wide receiver

"A fun situation for a guard is having a twelve-play drive where we run and pass the ball all the way down the field and end the drive by scoring a touchdown! Through physical run blocking and protecting the quarterback, the running backs and the wide receivers can make all those spectacular plays that all the fans love so much. The crowd definitely is not cheering directly for us, the guards, but our teammates all realize that the offensive success happens because of us, the offensive line."

—Guard Brad Badger, Minnesota Vikings

Tackles and **guards** are **offensive linemen**. Basically, all of these offensive linemen have the same jobs or assignments. They are not eligible to receive the ball. Instead, their assignment on the field is to block. They block incoming defensive players by using their arms, hands, or whole bodies to stop, push, or shove defensive players out of the way. They attempt to reroute an incoming defensive player in order to make a hole for the ball carrier, or to clear a path, a **running lane**, for the ball carrier. Sometimes the linemen set a **screen**. They move downfield to block for the receiver who catches the ball behind the line of scrimmage. The receiver *must* catch the ball or the linemen downfield will get a penalty for **illegal receivers downfield**.

Another offensive lineman assignment is to block the incoming defensive players so they cannot reach the quarterback while he is trying to pass the ball to a player downfield. They try to protect the quarterback from getting sacked or from getting rushed to throw the ball too quickly before the player downfield is in position to catch the ball.

The linemen's main job is to block, but it must be done a certain way. He cannot grab and hold onto a defensive player or onto the player's clothing or he will be penalized for **holding**.

Back to my dear sister. If you watch any football at all, you will invariably hear the term "holding" used quite frequently. My sister heard it over and over. Finally, she asked, "I don't get it. What are they holding?" The possibilities seem endless. In this instance, the term means that one player was illegally holding onto another player. It could be his arm, the jersey, or any part of him. You can push, shove, grab, block, tackle, but mercy, mercy, don't hold!

Holding results in a ten-yard penalty that is measured from the point on the field where the holding took place. Another penalty that may be called on offensive linemen is **clipping**. Unless the play is within a few yards of the end zone, an offensive lineman cannot block a defensive player from behind; this is called clipping. The defensive player needs to be able to see the block coming; this rule reduces potential injury to the defensive players. Clipping warrants a fifteen-yard penalty. (The more serious the action, the bigger the penalty!)

Holding

Once the defense lines up for a play, the center takes note of the type of defensive formation that is used and gives the offensive linemen last minute directions for the play. Remember, the offense must have seven men on the line, but the defense is not required to have a specific number of players on the line. On some plays, the offensive linemen may **double team** one of the defensive players: two offensive linemen may be assigned to cover one defensive player who poses a threat to the offensive plan. Double teaming may be used for both pass plays and running plays. Offensive linemen may also be assigned to block in a zone (a specific area) or "block man-to-man." Minor adjustments on the offense occur within a few short seconds before the ball is snapped and the play begins.

E. The Wide Receivers

"The best part of being a wide receiver is the challenge it provides. Typically, the wide receiver is out there, one-on-one, with the defensive back. If the wide receiver can beat the defensive back, then there is little between him and the end zone!"

—Wide Receiver Troy Walters (Recipient of the 1999 Biletnikoff Award as the nation's best receiver), Minnesota Vikings

During a tailgate on one pleasant fall day, I was talking to a lady who had just started attending football games. She obviously had some familiarity with football because she knew some of the lingo. In the course of our chitchat, she said, " I am curious about one thing. How often does a receiver intercept the ball?" Oh, dear. When I responded, "Well, *never*," she shot a look my way that matched her question: confused. I told her how an interception occurs when a defensive player jumps in and catches the ball that was intended for the receiver. In other words, the intended receiver "got beat." A defensive player outran him, out-smarted him, or simply got to the ball before it reached the hands of the receiver. Interceptions turn the ball over to the other team. She said, "Thanks. I'm glad I didn't ask that question in front of a lot of people."

The **wide receivers** (also called **wide outs**) are the offensive players whose main job is to catch (receive) the ball when it is thrown to them and to run *fast* with the ball to gain as many yards as possible. The wide receivers may line up in several different positions, depending on the offensive play that is called and depending on the number of wide receivers used for a given play. Usually one receiver will start on the line of scrimmage. You can tell the wide receiver by the way he positions himself wide, or away from the other players on the line of scrimmage. He is the player out there by himself.

The only players on the line of scrimmage that are eligible to receive a pass are the players that are on the ends; the other five players on the line of scrimmage can only block. If a tight end, one of the eligible receivers, is not used, there will be two wide receivers, one on each end of the line of scrimmage.

The term **wide receiver** is a general term used for players who are skilled at running to catch passes and then running fast to get as many yards as possible. The term **split end** is a name given to a wide receiver who lines up on the line of scrimmage. He is on the "end" of the line of scrimmage and he is "split" away from the rest of the men on the line of scrimmage, hence the name.

Wide receivers who are not placed on the line of scrimmage will line up a yard or more behind the line of scrimmage. The term **flanker** is a name given to the wide receiver who is behind the line of scrimmage.

As soon as the ball is snapped, the receivers take off running downfield. They have specific **pass routes** that they

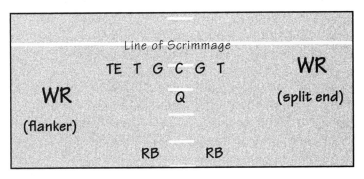

C = Center
G = guard
Q = quarterback
RB = running back

T = tackle
TE = tight end
WR = wide receiver

try to run so the quarterback knows exactly where they will be on the field as the play unfolds. The receivers, however, have to fend off the defensive players who are "in their faces" trying to knock them off course, force them out of bounds, or disrupt their timing so they won't be in position to catch a pass. If **man-to-man coverage** is used by the defense, one defensive player will try to stay close to one particular receiver to prevent him from catching the ball or running with the ball if the pass is caught. Double teaming may also be used on a strong receiver; two defensive players are assigned to cover the receiver and "shut him down" by not allowing him to make plays. If **zone coverage** is used by the defense, defensive players are assigned to cover a particular area of the field and tackle the ball carrier when he enters their zone. You will learn more about these defensive tactics in the next chapter.

No question is a dumb question, right? After all, how else can a person learn the game of football? Most games have at least one penalty called for "interference." During a game that was loaded with interference calls, the lady next to me commented, "Did he get in the way again?" I asked her what she meant. "Well, that ref is always getting called for interference. What's he interfering with? Why doesn't he stay out of the way?" Trying not to laugh, I simply said, "He called the interference. He didn't do it himself." "Oh," she said. "So, who interfered with what? The play? The clock? What?" This is a good time to explain this call.

The receivers must be given the opportunity to get in position to catch a pass. A **pass interference** penalty is called if a defensive player makes contact with the receiver before the receiver catches the ball or if he interferes with the receiver's opportunity to get in position to catch the pass. Trying to push the receiver out of the path of the ball or trying to hit or knock the receiver's arm or hand so he can't catch the ball draws the interference call. In the NFL, the penalty is an **automatic first down** (a new set of four attempts for the offense to move the ball ten yards) at the place where the violation occurred. In high school and college, a pass interference is a fifteen-yard penalty and a first down. In all levels of football, this penalty is a huge advantage for the offense.

Pass interference will not be called on the defensive player if the defensive player has his head turned, has his eye on the ball, and is clearly making his own attempt to catch the ball. The defensive player has an equal opportunity to go after the ball for an **interception**. Interestingly, an interference call may also be called on the receiver if the receiver hits or pushes the defensive player out of the way in order to prevent him from intercepting the ball.

Pass Interference

When you watch NFL games on TV, you'll hear announcers use some odd-sounding expressions. One that I found most interesting was, "One knee equals two feet." That sounds like one strange creature! This expression means that a player must have control of the ball in bounds in order for the play to be considered a completed pass. If the receiver is tackled or falls near the sideline, the play is good if the player's knee touches the ground in bounds or if both feet are in bounds—even if the rest of the body falls out of bounds. If only one foot was inbounds, the pass is incomplete. (There is one exception. If the receiver catches the ball in the air but is tackled or pushed out of bounds, the refs will rule the pass as completed if the receiver's feet most likely would have landed in bounds if he had not be tackled in midair. This is a tricky call.) So, for the pass to be complete, one knee or two feet have to touch in bounds. The next time you see this happen, yell, "It's good. One knee equals two feet!" You may astound your friends.

Incomplete

In the NFL, a pass is complete when the receiver catches the ball, has both feet in bounds, and has control of the ball. In high school and college, the receiver has to have only one foot in bounds for a pass to be ruled complete. A ball caught out of bounds is ruled as an **incomplete pass**. If the pass is incomplete, the offense did not make any yards on that play and they begin a new down on the same line of scrimmage as the last down. If the pass is complete, the play ends when the receiver is tackled, fumbles, or slips and falls.

When the quarterback intends to call a running play instead of a passing play, one of the receivers may be assigned to run down the field to trick the defense into thinking that the ball will be thrown downfield. More frequently, when the quarterback calls a running play, the receivers are assigned the job of blocking for the running backs. They try to keep the defensive players out of the running lane intended for the running back to move with the ball.

F. The Tight End

The **tight end** (another type of receiver) is part of the offensive line on the line of scrimmage. Unlike the wide receivers, the tight end is close to or "tight to" the other offensive linemen. The side of the field that the tight end is on is called the **strong side** of the offense. The other end of the line of scrimmage where there is no tight end is called the **weak side** of the line of scrimmage. The tight end may go out for a pass (work as a receiver) or he may be assigned the job of blocking to prevent the defense from interfering with the running or the passing play. Because tight ends do more blocking than receiving, they are often bigger than wide receivers. For some offensive formations (such as the Run and Shoot offense), you will notice that no tight end is used. Instead, another wide receiver is placed on the line instead of the tight end.

> "I love the tight end position because, in my opinion, it demands the most versatile athlete on the football field. The tight end has to be big, strong, and tenacious enough to block defensive linemen in the trenches and yet fast, light-footed, and sure-handed enough to beat smaller defensive backs and then make the big plays by catching passes."
> -Tight End Greg Clark, San Francisco 49ers

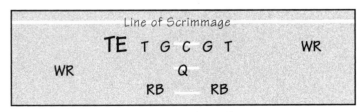

```
                 Line of Scrimmage
         TE  T  G  C  G  T              WR

   WR                    Q

                   RB      RB
```

C = center   T = tackle
G = guard   TE = tight end
Q = quarterback   WR = wide receiver
RB = running back

G. The Running Backs

The power of running backs makes them a great joy to watch. In high school, Kailee, who was large and strong for his age, was a running back. He would tuck that ball under his arm and plow off downfield. Sometimes he dragged a few players with him and kept on going. This was a far cry from earlier years. The father of one of Kailee's best friends actually kept videotapes dating back to the boys' flag football years. When Kailee signed his intent for Stanford, one of the coaches at North Eugene and his friend's father spliced together footage that spanned the years. One of the most delightful clips showed Kailee in flag football running with the ball held way out to the side, totally unprotected. All it would have taken was one fast player to run up and swipe the ball from his outstretched hand. It didn't happen, but it could have. Eventually Kailee learned to tuck that ball close to his body so it couldn't get ripped out from his hold very easily. When you watch the great running backs, you'll see that it's a downright miracle that they manage to hang onto that ball the way they do. 'Tis not an easy feat when players come after them from every direction with a fierce determination to end the play.

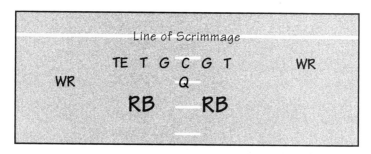

C = center
G = guard
Q = quarterback
RB = running back

T = tackle
TE = tight end
WR = wide receiver

The running backs do what their title indicates: they start off behind the line of scrimmage and they run with the ball. When the ball is handed to a running back, as opposed to being thrown to a wide receiver or a tight end, he tucks the ball under his arm and **rushes** (runs) to gain as many yards as possible. A running back has other players blocking and trying to make "holes" for him to run through, but remember that the defensive players are doing everything they can to get to the ball carrier. Though the goal is to move the ball forward, you will often see fancy footwork and darting running paths as the running back tries to weave his way through the defensive players. The game clock continues to tick when the running back is tackled in bounds. The clock stops if he fumbles or runs out of bounds. The **rushing yards** in a game show the number of yards the ball was moved in running plays. When the offensive play is not a running play, the running backs protect the quarterback by blocking the incoming defensive players, or they may also run down the field to catch the pass.

> "The running back position is the centerpiece of durability. A running back has to be durable in order to succeed, whether he is lead blocking or carrying the ball. A running back must be in tune with his own body and all of his movements as well as the entire field of play."
> —Running Back Obafemi Ayanbadejo, Baltimore Ravens

The term "running back" is a general term used for fullbacks and halfbacks (also called tailbacks). The **fullbacks** at times run and catch the ball, but most of the time they block defensive players to help make a running lane for the other running back, the halfback. A **halfback** or **tailback**, whose main job is to get the ball and run, is often smaller and quicker than the fullbacks. Different offensive formations are used, so the running backs don't always line up the same way on each play. In an **I Formation**, the letter "I" is formed by the center, quarterback, fullback, and half-back lining up one behind the other. A **T formation** is when the fullback and the halfback are positioned behind the quarterback, one a few yards to the right, the other a few yards to the left. Since the backs are split apart in this formation, they are called **split backs**. The I formation and the T formation are two possible formations for the running backs, but others are also used.

Running backs see a lot of action. I often heard the term "smashmouth football." Until I was informed otherwise, I thought it referred to the intimidating, "get in your head" kind of chatter that some players are notorious for on the field. You know, the kind of "your mama" talk designed to undermine the other player's concentration and to take his mind off the game. But, I was wrong. It has nothing to do with trash talking. "Smashmouth football" refers to games in which the offense keeps calling running play after running play and passes are kept to a minimum. This is the kind of game where the running backs really work their "tails" (their backs?) off. They undergo direct contact, tackles, and hard hitting for a series of plays. Fortunately, the term does not need to be taken literally; the mouth guards and the face masks on their helmets protect their mouths.

The following are other common terms related to running backs:

1. **The sweep**—Remember that the running back usually has to face an onslaught of defensive players, and he has to find a way to get through the defensive line if he is going to make some yardage. Sometimes the running back intends to get the ball and run as far upfield as possible and then to head toward the sidelines to get out of bounds. The other players who are blocking for him

know when this play is called and will try to form a wall to protect the runner so he can carry the ball forward and "sweep" to the side of the field.

2. **Stats**—The statistics for running backs tell the number of rushing yards (how many yards they carried the ball) and the **average yards per carry** (an average distance they were able to carry the ball).

3. **The Draw Play**—You learned about the Play-Action-Pass in part B of this chapter: the quarterback fakes by pretending to give the ball to a running back but then actually drops back to pass. The Draw Play is the opposite; this time the quarterback drops back to give the appearance that he is going to pass, but instead of passing, he hands the ball off to a running back. These fake plays often catch the defense off guard and force them to react and move in a certain direction. They lose momentum, which gives the offense a little more time to make the play work.

Media coverage for football often focuses on the quarterback, the receivers, and the running backs. One might assume that these are "the most important players" on the offense. A game usually won't be won if the quarterback lacks the skills to orchestrate plays, lacks a strong arm, is inexperienced in the position, or is unable to provide strong leadership for the team. Frequently, the quarterback receives the glory for a win or the brunt of criticism for a loss. Many of the spectacular plays are performed by the receivers and the tight end, and media highlights favor plays made by these players. The "work horses" on the offense are often the running backs. They run into the thick of things on the field, so when they gain good yardage, their work is appreciated and spotlighted, too. The truth, however, is that every single player on the offense is important. If the center, the guards, and the tackles don't do their jobs, the quarterback will be ineffective, the running backs won't get the help they need to find running room, and the receivers will not be able to break free from the defense or get in position to catch the ball. Every player is significant. Every player contributes to both the wins and the losses. Football is a team sport.

4
DEFENSIVE
PLAYERS

My nephew Charles, his wife Julie, and their two children Jennelle and Chris often joined me and my sister at the Stanford games. Being true "family fans," our eyes were often more focused on Kailee than on any of the other players. If Kailee wasn't on the field, everyone would be asking, "Where is he? Why isn't he out there? Is there something wrong?" Now when I watch some of the Vikings games from Oregon, the television cameras often are not on the part of the field that I want to see. "Where is Kailee? Why is he off the field? Is something wrong?" Finally I have learned to take a more relaxed attitude because I know that defensive coordinators call many kinds of defensive plays and defensive formations. Each defensive play and each defensive formation require different combinations of players. Players are rotated in and out because of the playbook. With time and a little practice, you can recognize some of the different defensive combinations by watching which players are on the field together and which players leave the field together. Of course, as soon as you think you have recognized a specific pattern of players on the field, new combinations are implemented. After all, part of the game involves outsmarting the opponent and keeping the game plan unpredictable!

A. Basic Defensive Formation

The defense, as you now know, consists of eleven play-ers. The goal of the defense is to stop the offensive team from moving the ball forward and from scoring. Unlike the offense, which always has seven players on the line of scrimmage, the number of defensive players on the line of scrimmage will vary depending on the defensive formation for each play. One common defensive formation, the **4-3 defense**, places four defensive linemen on the line of scrimmage and three linebackers behind them, behind the line of scrimmage. This basic 4-3 defense is shown in the following chart.

The players on the line of scrimmage are called the **defensive linemen**. They line up opposite the offensive line-men. The linemen squat down or bend over at the line of scrimmage and have one hand or their fingertips in the dirt. **Defensive tackles** line up to face the offense's center or the

Basic Defense Chart

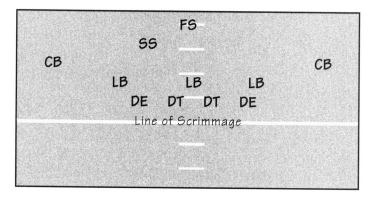

CB = cornerback   FS = free safety
DE = defensive end   LB = linebacker
DT = defensive tackle   SS = strong safety

offense's guards. Two **defensive ends** will line up on each end of the line of scrimmage to face the offense's tackles.

Behind the **defensive** linemen are the **linebackers**. As indicated by their names, they are *back* or behind the line of scrimmage. A defensive formation may use three linebackers: a strong outside linebacker, a middle linebacker, and a weak outside linebacker. The linebackers begin a play in a more upright or standing position.

During lunch one day at work, the talk shifted to football. Two of the people at the table loved to talk football; the other two couldn't have cared less. One of the men commented that his team probably wouldn't do well this year because of their "weak secondary." One of the non-football fans commented, "I don't have a clue what you guys are talking about. What do you mean secondary? Are those the guys that are second on the field?" Another person responded, "I think they are the second string, the guys who don't get out and start the game." Who do you think was right? Read on to find out what secondary really means.

The rest of the defensive team is called the **secondary**. Depending on the defensive formation used for a play, the secondary may consist of two cornerbacks, one strong safety, and one free safety.

Because the defense's main purpose is to stop the offense from moving the ball forward, the statistics that are shown for defensive players focus on the number of tackles, assists, sacks, and interceptions. Credit for a tackle is given when a defensive player tackles and stops any offensive player who has the ball. **Tackles for a loss** means that not only was there a tackle, but the tackle occurred behind the line of scrimmage so the offense lost yards on the play. You will notice on many plays that more than one defensive player may be involved in stopping the player with the ball; an **assist** occurs when two or more defensive players together tackle and stop the ball carrier. Credit for a sack is given when a defensive player tackles the quarterback when he still has the ball behind the line of scrimmage. If two defensive players **sack** the quarterback together, each defensive player is given a half a sack for the statistics.

B. The Defensive Linemen

Remember my comments about the huge offensive line—the guards and the tackles? Well, the defensive linemen are the ones who get to see the whites of the eyes of the big guys. Needless to say, the defensive linemen need to have size, power, speed, and agility to live up to this challenge. Watch what happens when these guys face each other at the beginning of each play!

The defensive linemen's main job is to stop the offensive play from developing. They try to stop the offense's blocking plan, prevent a ball carrier from getting the ball and running, or put pressure on the quarterback so he can't make a play. When you hear that a team "stopped the run," you know that the defensive linemen had a great game and were able to prevent the running backs from gaining many yards (rushing yards). A defensive tackle who is lined up across from the offense's center is called a **nose tackle**. His job is to push the center back as soon as the ball is snapped

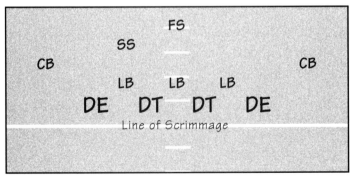

CB = cornerback   FS = free safety
DE = defensive end   LB = linebacker
DT = defensive tackle   SS = strong safety

> "The defensive linemen epitomize the essence of the game of football. It is primal, instinctual. It all goes back to the caveman days when one man came in and had to go face to face with another man. It is an offensive lineman versus a defensive lineman battling with all their strength whether it is for an inch or for a quarterback sack."
>
> -Defensive Lineman Carl Hansen, NY Giants

and to cover a gap that may be used for a player to run through with the ball. The defensive ends are often the defensive linemen who try to get to the quarterback to disrupt the play or to force him to move out of the pocket (the area protected by an offensive "wall" of players). They may try to **rush** the quarterback so that his play doesn't work. The defensive end who is extremely quick to move off the line of scrimmage and reach the quarterback is called a pass rusher.

If one or more defensive linemen break through the offensive line to reach and tackle the quarterback while he still has the ball behind the line of scrimmage, the quarterback is **sacked**. The result is that the offensive team loses yardage, which requires the offense to make even more yards on the next down.

At Stanford, Kailee was a pass rusher and a defensive end. Throughout his four years at Stanford, Kailee always had a lot of fan support from his family and friends. Kailee's coaches were sometimes stunned by the size of the Wong contingency that gathered for games. One photographer from a Stanford newspaper who wanted to capture the "gang," found that he had to back up farther and farther to fit everyone in the picture. Friends, sisters, cousins, nephews, nieces, aunts, uncles, and every other conceivable relation from my side and the Hawaiian side of the family frequently gathered for the games. Often we all wore T-shirts or sweatshirts designed and silkscreened specifically for us by Carl, my neighbor in Eugene. Ah, we did have a lot of fun. Great comraderie and lasting friendships also developed among the parents who faithfully gathered for games. We traveled to North Carolina, to Memphis for the Liberty Bowl, and to El Paso for the Sun Bowl, not to mention the trips within Pac-10 territory and the Hula Bowl in Maui. It wasn't always easy, but I became an expert on hunting down airfare bargains, gathering frequent flyer miles, and economizing. Some may think tromping around the country for football games is crazy, but the trips became my greatest source of entertainment. After all, every woman has to have her priorities, and mine were (and are) football!

C. The Linebackers

If you really want to get confused (and feel totally ignorant), take a look at the diagrams in a linebacker's playbook. Guaranteed, you will not believe the number of defensive packages, or "coverages" that players have to memorize. To top it all off, each play has a special code name! One player lines up a little bit more to the right, and bang, the lineup has a new name! The task of memorizing the meaning of this coded language becomes easier as players become seasoned through years of playing.

Defensive coordinators call most of the plays from the sidelines. The plays are sent onto the field through a complicated system of hand signals. Unlike the quarterback, no one on the defense has a handy headphone inside his helmet to receive the calls. The plays are announced quickly; players need to mentally associate the code names to the position and assignment they are to perform during the play. Intellect does play a crucial role!

> "The linebacker unit is the center of the defense. Linebackers are asked to take on 320-pounders as well as help on coverage against extremely quick wide receivers. On the snap of the ball, linebackers have to be ready to move many different directions, depending on the action of the offense. It's great and can be a lot of fun."
> -Linebacker Kailee Wong, Minnesota Vikings

Linebackers have a wide variety of responsibilities and need to be ready to react to many different offensive plays. The job of linebackers is to stop (tackle) any offensive player who is running with the ball (who got past the defensive linemen) or to drop back on the field to be ready to cover any wide receivers who may be running downfield to catch a pass. The linebackers also watch for opportunities to make an interception, to catch a pass that was intended

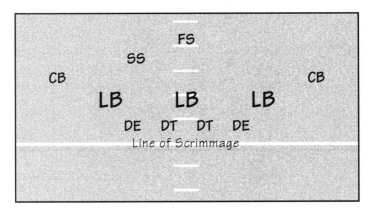

CB = cornerback
DE = defensive end
DT = defensive tackle

FS = free safety
LB = linebacker
SS = strong safety

for an offensive player. When a pass play is expected, the defense may call for a **blitz,** which means a linebacker joins the defensive linemen on the line of scrimmage. The goal is to rush in and to put pressure on the quarterback, or better yet, to sack the quarterback.

A common defensive formation is to use three linebackers: a strong outside linebacker, a middle linebacker, and a weak outside linebacker. Teams often create "cute" names for the different linebackers. For example, the linebacker that positions himself across from the tight end is called the **strong outside linebacker** or "Sam," because it begins with the letter "s." Because the tight end may be designated to receive a pass, the strong outside linebacker tries to disrupt the path the tight end plans to run to get into position to receive the ball. The strong outside linebacker may also be used as a pass rusher, in which case he needs to use an explosive burst of energy and speed to get to the quarterback, or he may move back in the field to defend a pass play further down the field.

One player, not realizing his mom didn't understand the mysterious coded language, bubbled with excitement when he said, "I don't want to be Sam or Willie, I want to be Mike!" His mother, like so many mothers, responded, "Honey, just be yourself. You have a lot of talent and need to learn to have confidence in who you are." I wonder if this mom ever understood that her son wanted to be the middle linebacker, or "Mike," who is the boss of the defense, the guy who keys in on the offensive formation in a split second and then calls out any defensive changes to the rest of the players. Every team has a Sam, a Willie, and a Mike, and yes, they are close buddies on the field.

The **middle linebacker** may be nicknamed Mike ("m" for middle linebacker). The middle linebacker is the defensive player who announces the defensive plays to use for different situations on the field. He tries to interpret the kind of offense that is set up on the field and to coordinate the defensive efforts. He frequently yells out changes or warnings to the other defensive players who may not be in the right position to see sudden offensive changes. His other main responsibility is to try to tackle the ball carrier.

The **weak outside linebacker** may be named Will or Willie ("w" for weak), but he is far from weak. The responsibilities of the weak outside linebacker vary with the defensive play that is called. He defends his side of the field, may be used as a pass rusher, or may drop back to defend the backfield.

The personal statistics for linebackers show the number of tackles per game. A **tackle** means that the defensive player brought the ball carrier to the ground without anyone else's help (no assists). If the linebackers don't tackle the ball carrier, there is only one line of defense left to prevent the ball carrier from scoring: the secondary.

Football is full of myths. One myth that I personally love to de-
bunk is the myth that football players are "all brawn and no
brain." Nothing could be further from the truth! I have learned
to appreciate the amount of intellect and concentration that
are needed to learn the contents of playbooks, understand and
execute complex strategies, interpret action on the field, predict possible actions and reactions of other players, and main-
tain a focused and alert mind throughout both routine
practices and entire games. The mind is constantly churning
and continually making associations between codes, symbols,
diagrams, players, the playing field, and the body.

D. Basics about the Secondary

The **secondary** is the term used for the defensive players positioned in the back of the field. For this reason, they are also called **defensive backs**. Their job is to defend the backfield from any pass plays and to prevent the ball carrier from getting into the end zone. They are the last line of defense; it is crucial that they stop any ball carrier who manages to break through the defensive line and the linebackers. If an offensive player with the ball makes it past the secondary, there is no defense left between the ball carrier and the end zone.

A common defensive formation uses two cornerbacks, a strong safety, and a free safety; however, different defensive formations may use more than four defensive backs. If a fifth defensive back is used, he is called the **nickel back**. If six defensive backs are used, the sixth man is called the **dime back**.

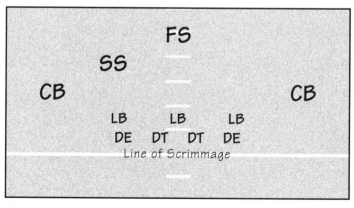

CB = cornerback   FS = free safety
DE = defensive end   LB = linebacker
DT = defensive tackle   SS = strong safety

As previously discussed in the section on wide receivers, the secondary may be assigned to man-to-man coverage or zone coverage. Man-to-man coverage occurs when a defensive back is assigned to cover one specific offensive player (a running back, a wide receiver, or a tight end.) The defensive back's job is to stay with that one specific player and disrupt any play, regardless of where the player moves on the field. In zone coverage, each defensive back is assigned to defend a specific part of the backfield by being ready to tackle any ball carrier who comes into his zone. The defensive backs watch the quarterback to try to predict the type of play that will be used and the direction the ball will be thrown or run. Meanwhile, the offense does not always know the kind of defense that is planned. Sometimes the quarterback tries to find out by sending **a man in motion**. One man, usually a running back, a wide receiver, or a tight end, begins running parallel to the line of scrimmage before the ball is snapped. (Yes, this is legal, but only *one* man may be put in motion.) If a defensive back starts moving to cover the man in motion, the quarterback knows that man-to-man coverage is planned. As you can see, the strategies in football are complex and always involve efforts on the part of the offense and the defense to try to discover ways to outdo, outsmart, and overpower each other.

Many big plays can be made during a game by the defensive backs. When a ball is passed, both the offensive receiver and a defensive player may go after the ball. As previously discussed, interceptions occur when a defensive player catches a pass that was intended for the receiver. However, the defensive player will receive a pass interference penalty if he bumps, hits, or makes the slightest

Pass Interference

contact with the intended receiver while the ball is in the air. More often, defensive backs will try to break up a pass by jumping up and **deflecting the ball** so it never reaches the hands of the receiver. A fumble, when the ball carrier loses the ball, can be forced by the defensive backs (or any defensive player), or the ball may be **stripped** by a defensive player pulling the ball out of the hands of the ball carrier.

E. The Cornerbacks

> "The best thing about playing corner is competing with the guys running down the field, one-on-one. The corner is the island, and all the eyes and the pressure are on the cornerback. This is the style I like!"
>
> —Cornerback Robert Tate, Minnesota Vikings

The cornerbacks are the "defensive backs" in the secondary who are in the back corners of the defensive formation, positioned away from the linebackers or defensive ends. Their exact positions vary depending on the defensive game plan. Cornerbacks are *fast* and ready to challenge the wide receivers. In man-to-man coverage, they generally line up directly across from the wide receivers and stay with that receiver no matter where he moves on the field. The cornerbacks cover the wide receivers whether they are coming down the field to catch a pass or have already caught a pass and are running downfield toward the goal line with the ball. The cornerback may also try to beat the wide receiver to the ball for an interception that will cause a **turnover**.

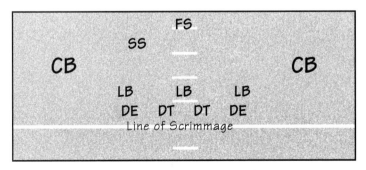

CB = cornerback   FS = free safety
DE = defensive end   LB = linebacker
DT = defensive tackle   SS = strong safety

F. The Safeties

On one occasion in the earlier years, my sister asked why Kailee didn't stand further back in the field. I told her that is where the safeties are positioned, and Kailee isn't a safety. "Safety? What's that? Is it like a safety valve or a safety net?" Yes, in many ways the safeties are "safety nets" or "safety valves." They try to keep the back part of the field safe from invasion.

> "The safety is the leader of the secondary. He's the last one with a chance to stop the ball carrier. If he doesn't make the play, the scoreboard will show the consequences."
>
> —Safety Anthony Bass, Minnesota Vikings

The main job of the **strong safety** is to tackle, and to tackle hard. The strong safety lines up on the "strong side of the field," meaning he stands directly across from the tight end who may run out for a pass play. When the strong safety defends

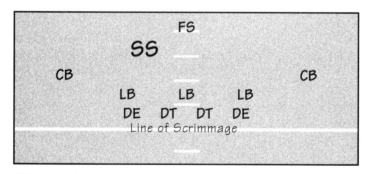

CB = cornerback
DE = defensive end
DT = defensive tackle

FS = free safety
LB = linebacker
SS = strong safety

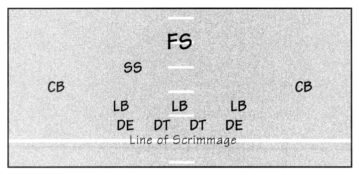

CB = cornerback   FS = free safety
DE = defensive end   LB = linebacker
DT = defensive tackle   SS = strong safety

against a pass, he drops into pass coverage. When the strong safety is assigned to cover the tight end to prevent him from moving downfield with the ball, he is using man-to-man coverage. Other times, the strong safety is assigned to zone coverage, to defend one area of the field and tackle any ball carrier who comes into his zone. Because the strong safety is farther back in the field, he is often able to watch the play develop and sense the effectiveness of the defensive line and the linebackers in stopping a given play. He needs to be able to defend the backfield against both running plays and pass plays.

The **free safety** is the last defensive player in the back of the field. If a ball carrier gets past the other defensive players, the free safety is the team's last chance to stop the ball. If a ball carrier gets past the free safety, the ball carrier will often *hit his head on the goal post,* which means he will score a touchdown! The free safety may *play deep,* which means he stays far in the backfield to defend against a long pass. He may also use his speed to run up the field to fill in a gap where no other defensive player is available. When man-to-man coverage is used, the free safety may be the one defensive back that is not assigned to cover a specific player. He remains free to cover any part of the field that needs extra defense. A free safety may be assigned the job of a cornerback (to cover the receivers) if the offense uses three receivers for a play.

If at times you feel a little overwhelmed by all the terms, remember that they become more familiar and understandable as you watch more games. It is easy to understand how the meaning of some football terms get distorted, even if you know something about the game. For example, a friend once asked me a remarkably confusing question. He asked, "Is the safety in a safe zone when he scores a safety?" Oh dear! Where to begin! Remember, the term "safety" has two completely different meanings. The backfield defensive player (a safety) is not the same player who scores a safety. A two-point safety is scored when an offensive player is caught with the ball in the wrong end zone. The offensive ball carrier who was caught in his own end zone doesn't score points for his own team; in fact, he actually gives points to the other team! Consequently, the area that he is in when he is caught with the ball is really not safe at all! In fact, it's a danger zone! (Hey, I didn't make up these terms. Don't roll your eyes at me!) My friend, needless to say, responded, "Oh, I knew that. I was just testing you."

5
SPECIAL TEAMS

"What??? There's more? How many more positions do I need to learn about if there are six more teams involved?" Relax. The special teams are a little different than the offensive and the defensive teams which have names for every position. The discussion here will focus on the basics. When you watch the special teams come onto the field, you will notice that many of the players on the special teams also play on the offensive team or the defensive team. Many players have these dual roles. Not only do they learn the playbooks for their main position, but they also learn the playbooks for special teams. Salutes to the strong minds and the strong bodies!

Four of the special teams are "transition teams." These teams are on the field when the ball "changes" hands or is turned over to the other team. The transition teams are the **kick off team**, the **kick off return team**, the **punt team**, and the **punt return team**. The remaining two teams are involved in scoring attempts. The **PAT kicking team** tries to score a point after a touchdown and score points by kicking field goals. The **PAT blocking team** tries to prevent the other team from scoring.

A. The Kick Off Team

The **kick off team** is the team that kicks the ball to the other team at the beginning of each half of the game, after a touchdown is scored, when the PAT (point-after-a-touchdown, or two-point conversion) is attempted, and after a field goal is kicked.

Ten players and a place kicker make up the offensive kick off team. During a kick off, the ball is placed on a kick off tee on the 30-yard line (35-yard line for college and 40-yard line for high school). The place kicker lines up seven or eight feet behind the ball. The remaining ten players form one line across the field with five players on each side of the kicker.

When the whistle blows, the kicker takes his well-planned steps toward the ball and kicks the ball downfield as far as possible. The longer the kick, the more yardage the kick off return team will have to cover before reaching the end zone to score. As soon as the kicker begins moving, the line of ten men begins running forward in unison. They are allowed to run past the line of scrimmage as soon the kicker

PK = place kicker
X = players on the kick off team

makes contact with the ball. The line of men, each having a lane, or path to run to reach the receiver, gains as much speed and momentum as possible to get downfield to cover the ball (stop the receiver with the ball).

As they charge down the field, they meet the kick off return team coming at them full speed. The kick off return players try to block the kick off team (coverage team), to knock them out of the way to make a path for the ball carrier to run, and to keep them from ending the play by reaching and tackling the ball carrier. The main goal of the kick off team is to tackle the ball carrier as far back in the field as possible. Kick offs are fast, loaded with action, and downright exciting!

During the kick off, the first ten yards past the line of scrimmage are significant. If the ball is kicked at least ten yards, a player on the kick off team can recover the ball. If the ball goes out of bounds before it travels ten yards, or if a player on the kick off team touches the ball before it travels ten yards, a five-yard penalty results, and the ball is re-kicked. If the kick is short and goes out of bounds after it travels ten yards, the other team gains possession of the ball at that yard line.

During a kick off toward the end of one game, my sister commented, "Man, he sure blew that one! What happened to him anyway?" I asked what she meant because the kicker did exactly what I had anticipated. She said, "Well, usually the kicks are way up in the air and long. That one hardly went anywhere." Later, as she became more seasoned, she knew when to expect the short kick offs. Yes, she was most proud of herself! Continue on to learn about the onside kick and the wild scramble for the ball that takes place in split seconds.

An **onside kick** is an intentionally short kick that sometimes is used toward the end of the game by the team that is losing. With a short kick (at least ten yards), the kick off team hopes that the kick off return team will be caught off-guard, will not be ready to catch the ball, will fumble the ball, or that their own player will be able to get to the ball first. If the kick off team is successful, they keep possession of the ball and are given a new first down. If they are not successful, the opponent takes possession of the ball and has a much better field position because they only have about half of the field to cover to reach the end zone where they can score. The onside kick is a last ditch effort to keep the ball and have an opportunity to score.

B. The Kick Off Return Team

The **kick off return team**, an eleven-man team consisting of nine blockers and two kick returners, is positioned in the backfield to catch the kick off ball and to block the incoming players who want to stop the ball carrier. As soon as the kick off return team receives the ball, they become the offense. Unlike the kick off team that lines up along the line of scrimmage, the kick off return team is spread out on the field. The kick off return team sets up blocks to stop the incoming kick off team and creates a path for the kick returner to run with the ball as far downfield as possible toward the end zone.

One set of **blockers** initially runs backward, watching the oncoming players and selecting the best time to block them. If they can time the blocking precisely, they can create holes, or running paths for the ball carrier. Their goal is to get as many of the kick off team players out of the way.

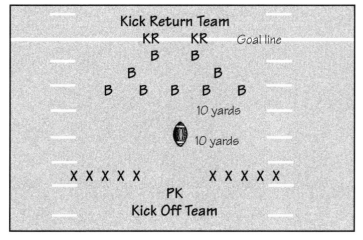

B = Blockers
KR = Kick returners

A second set of blockers sets up a barrier (a wedge-shaped line) to keep the oncoming players from ruining the path of the kick returner. The kick return team has done its job if the ball can be carried to at least the middle of the field.

Dead Ball

One or two players, *kick returners*, stay deep in the backfield, ready to catch the ball. If two kick returners are placed in the backfield, the returner who is not going after the ball helps block for the designated receiver (kick returner). Good kick returners have good hands for catching the ball, are fast, and can cut back and forth quickly to avoid the oncoming tacklers. Once the ball carrier is tackled, the ball is dead, and his offensive team comes on the field to begin a first down at the point where the ball was marked dead.

The kick off return team has to be prepared for a variety of situations that can occur. Kick offs are so unpredictable and exciting that fans are often on their feet to see how the play unfolds. Following are a few of the situations that might occur:

1. Sometimes a touchdown is scored on a kick off. This is the ultimate play for a kick return team. The ball carrier catches the ball, begins running, dodges the tackles, and, aided by his blockers, breaks through all the players on the opposing team, and runs the entire length of the field to score a touchdown! The fans go wild when a kick returner "runs it back for a touchdown."

2. A more likely play is that the kick returner is tackled before he gets to the middle of the field. Kick returners often gain ten to twenty yards, but to do that, they need to weave their way in and out of congested traffic. Running lanes are hard to find. They need to maneuver and cut their way through the pack to find space to run.

3. On some occasions, the returner catches the ball, has possession, and then fumbles. When the kick returner fumbles, the ball becomes a **live ball**. Players from both teams can go after the ball and run with it to pick up as many yards for their team as possible. Again, the ultimate play would be for the player who recovers the fumble to be able to run the ball into the end zone for a touchdown.

4. One additional scenario that may occur is a **touchback**. If the kick returner catches the ball and is then forced into the end zone with the ball, or if he catches a long ball in the end zone, rather than try to fight his way out of the end zone, the kick returner can **take a knee**, which means he puts his knee down and thereby stops the play. The ball is then moved to the 20-yard line to begin the first down. Remember, if the ball carrier is tackled in the wrong end zone, the other team scores a safety (two points).

Touchback

C. The Punt Team

Two other special transition teams, the **punt team** and the **punt return team** come on the field on a fourth down when the offense is unsuccessful in **converting a third down** (moving the ball the necessary ten yards to get a new first down.) The punt team is the team that punts (kicks) the ball to get rid of it on the fourth down. The punt return team is the team on the field preparing to receive the ball.

The appearance of the punting team on the field indicates that the offense is having problems moving the ball and **converting the third down**. When the punting team is on the field, you know that the offense is too far away to attempt a field goal. The punting team is also a sign that the defense is doing its job and "shutting down" the offense. Rather than turn the ball over to the other team in the middle of the field or closer to the other team's end zone, the offense opts to punt (kick) the ball as far downfield as possible to give the other team the worst possible field position. The other team will have to work a lot harder to get down the field to the end zone to score.

The punting team begins the play as an offensive team, punting the ball away on the fourth down. However, after the ball is snapped, caught by the punter and punted downfield, the punt team becomes a defensive team whose mission is to stop the other team (now the offense) from moving the ball downfield. At the end of the play, the punt teams leave the field and the regular offensive and defen-

> "The best thing about my position happens during the practices! While most of the other players on the team are out there running all over the field, we (the kickers) get to practice our specific skill in our area away from everyone else."
> —Punter Mitch Berger, Minnesota Vikings

sive teams come on the field to take over and begin the first down.

The punt team can line up in a variety of ways on the field. A basic lineup, the punt formation, is shown in the following chart. The **punter** (this special kind of kicker) is behind the other players. Unlike the *place kicker* for kick offs, the punter is not allowed to use a tee. Instead, he stands about fifteen yards behind the line of scrimmage and behind the center. The center snaps the ball (throws the ball quickly between his legs) to the punter. The punter must catch the ball, take a step or two, drop the ball to his kicking foot, and punt the ball without the ball touching the ground. The punter kicks the ball as far downfield as possible. A good punt is long and high; a high punt (good **hang time**) gives his players time to run down the field toward the punt receiver.

In addition to the center and the place kicker, there are nine other punt team players on the field. One player, the

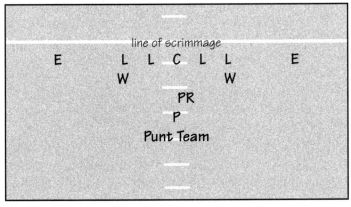

C = center   P = punter
E = ends   PR = protector
L = linemen   W = wings

"protector," may be positioned back by the punter to give the punter extra protection from the oncoming players. The linemen and the wings right behind the linemen try to block the oncoming players from reaching the punter and disrupting his punt or blocking his kick. The "ends" usually try to get down quickly to tackle the punt returner. Once the ball is punted, the punt team charges toward the punt returner to tackle him and to stop him from running with the ball.

The following are common terms you may hear when the punt teams are on the field.

1. **Corner Kick**—The punter may try to kick the ball toward the end zone but out of bounds. A great corner kick goes out of bounds on the 1- or the 2-yard line. The point where the ball goes out of bounds is marked (**spotted**) and the offensive team takes over at that point on the field. The offense then begins the battle to move the ball down the length of the field to reach the end zone to score.

2. **Returned Kick**—The receiving team's **punt returner** catches the ball and runs with it to get as many yards as possible before he is tackled. Sometimes the punt returner is able to find a path to run through all the defensive players and run the length of the field to score a touchdown. Usually, however, the punt returner is tackled before he can run that distance.

3. **Roll Dead**—The receiving team may not be in the right position to catch the ball, so they may decide not to even attempt a catch. Instead, the ball is left to bounce and roll until it comes to a stop or is stopped by a player. (This is the situation where you see a group of big men hovering over the ball, watching but not touching.) The punting team wants the ball to roll as far downfield as possible; the ball is dead as soon as a punting team

player touches it. Once the ball is ruled dead, the offense takes possession of the ball at the point it was spotted. When the ball is close to the end zone, the punt return team usually tries to avoid touching the ball because once the ball is touched by a punt return player, the ball is a live ball. If the punt returner fumbles the ball and an opposing player recovers the fumble, that player will not have far to go to score.

4. **Touchback**—A touchback occurs when the punter kicks the ball so far that it goes into his own end zone. The opposing team usually does not try to catch the ball and run with it because, in this instance, the ball will automatically be placed on the 20-yard line to begin a first down for the offense. As kickers refined their skills, touchbacks became more common. In 1999, the NFL started using a separate ball for kicking. The new balls used for kicking have not been "seasoned" or softened up. Some kickers are still able to belt the ball into the end zone, but the number of touch-

Touchback

backs and the accuracy of the kickers have been affected by this rule.

5. **Fake Punt**—Remember that punting is the last offensive play on a fourth down. Occasionally, you will see the offense attempt to trick the defense into believing the ball will be punted. However, the play is switched and the ball is either handed off to an offensive player for a run play or it is passed downfield to a receiver. A fake punt is risky; if the offense doesn't make the necessary yards for a first down, the other team will gain possession of the ball at the yard line where the play ends.

6. **Dropped Snap**—Sometimes the center does a poor job of snapping the ball between his legs and shooting it back to the punter. If the center drops the ball, the ball is considered live and any player from either team can recover the ball. If the punt team does not recover the ball, the other team will gain possession of the ball which will be closer to its own end zone.

D. The Punt Return Team

"I don't get it. Why is that player waving his arm in the air instead of getting ready to take off with the ball?" my sister once asked. "Well, if you were the punt returner and you saw the powerhouses stampeding straight for you, and you didn't think the odds were much in your favor to run very far, your arm would likely be waving frantically high in the air," I responded. Usually fans want to see the punt returner take the chance and run with the ball, but sometimes a better decision is to call for a "fair catch."

The **punt return team** is spread out on the field ready for the ball to be punted their way. The punt return team has three main jobs: try to block the punt, protect the punt returner from incoming players, and make a path for the punt returner to run with the ball.

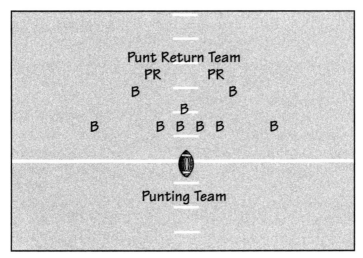

B = blockers
PR = punt returners

The following terms are related to the punt return team:

1. **Fair Catch**—If the punt returner decides that too many players are coming at him and it is unlikely that he will be able to run very far with the ball, he holds his arm above his head and waves to signal a fair catch. A fair catch means that the punt returner will not attempt to run with the ball. Players from the kicking team cannot tackle him; in fact, they must stay at least three feet away from the punt returner to give him a fair chance to catch the ball. If the player is tackled after he signals a fair catch, the kicking team is given a fifteen-yard penalty. If the ball is caught after signaling a fair catch, the ball is dead and spotted on that yard line. The offensive team begins playing with a first down at that point on the field.

2. **Punt Returned**— The punt returner catches the ball and runs down the field to gain as many yards as possible. Of course, to gain the yards, he will need to weave his way through the defensive players who come from all sides of the field with just one intention—to tackle him, to stop him in his tracks before he gains too many yards.

3. **Blocked Punt**—A **blocked punt** occurs when the punt return team sends players in to rush the kicker, throw his timing off, and try to block the kick from going very far down the field. Players may try to **deflect the ball** by tipping the ball while it is in the air. The main goal is to prevent the ball from moving farther down the field, that is, further away from the end zone that needs to be reached to score. However, if the punt is blocked and the ball does not cross the line of scrimmage, players from both teams can go after the ball, pick it up, and run. The offensive ball carrier (on the punt team) would still need to make the number of yards required for a first down to avoid turning the ball over to the other team.

4. **Muffed Ball**—If the punt returner *muffs* the ball (touches the ball but is not able to hold on to it or show controlled possession), players from either team can recover the loose ball. If a player from the kicking team recovers the ball, he cannot run with it; he **downs the ball** by *taking a knee* (putting his knee down to end the play). The ball becomes his team's ball at the point it was recovered.

5. As was previously mentioned, a **touchback** occurs when the punt lands in the end zone before any player touches it. A touchback also occurs when the punt returner catches the ball in the end zone, and *takes a knee* rather than trying to run out of the end zone with the ball. The ball is moved out to the 20-yard line on a touchback, so if a punt returner doesn't feel he can make it to the 20-yard line, it's wiser to *take a knee* and **down the ball**.

The punt team and the punt return team occupy the field for just this one down. As soon as the play is over, they hustle off the field to make room for the regular offense and the defense. The battle begins once again; the offense has four chances (downs) to move the ball ten yards or score. If they do not move the ball well on the third down, the punt teams will be back on the field for another "transition" play.

By now I hope you are getting a sense of the thrill in being a football fan! I laugh when I see the ridiculous commercials for "Football Widow Sales," assuming that the women of the world prefer shopping over watching football. Sheer nonsense!

E. The PAT Kicking Team

The **field goal** and the **PAT team** are both referred to as the **kicking team**. This team is used to score extra points (three for field goal and one for a point-after) by kicking the ball through the uprights.

The kicking team has a snapper, a holder and a place-kicker. The remaining players line up to block, to protect the kicker from the defensive blocking team. With one swift snap, the **snapper** (who is usually also the center), thrusts the ball through his legs to the **holder**. The holder stays in a kneeling position, ready to catch the snapped ball, turn it, and angle it the way the kicker wants it positioned. With one finger on the top of the ball, the holder holds the ball in place on the ground for the **placekicker** to kick. With one swift kick (hopefully before any defensive players get to him), the ball soars toward the goal post and the up-rights. All of this action takes place in a few very short sec-

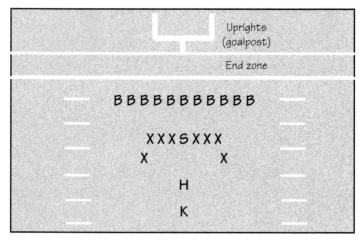

B = Blocking team   H = holder
X = kicking team players   K = kicker
s = snapper

onds. The points made by kicking teams often determine the winner of the game. If precise timing, perfect communication, and coordination are lacking between the snapper and the holder or the holder and the kicker, the chance of scoring points from kicking is greatly reduced.

The **field goal team** is called in on a fourth down when the offense is too far from the end zone for a touchdown, but is within field goal range, usually around the 30-yard line. Note, however, when the ball is placed on the 30-yard line, the kicker actually needs to kick more than thirty yards because the ball is kicked from seven yards behind the line of scrimmage, and the uprights (for the pros) are at the back of the ten-yard-wide end zone. So, a kick from the 30-yard line is really a forty-seven yard kick! In some games when the pressure to score is on and only a few seconds remain on the clock before the half or the end of the game, you will see field goal attempts made from even further back in the field.

If the offense is too far away from the end zone, but there's still ample time remaining on the clock for additional plays, a field goal attempt will not be made for one simple reason: if the kicker misses, the other team gets the ball at the point where the ball was kicked. (In high school, if the ball is kicked into the end zone but a field goal is not made, the ball is placed on the 20-yard line. If the ball does not reach the end zone, the offense takes over where the ball was downed.) That could be a huge advantage for the other team because they would get the ball closer to their own end zone for scoring. In this situation, rather than attempt a field goal, the offense would more likely opt to punt the ball. If little time is left on the clock before the end of the half or the end of the game, a team may attempt a long field goal as a last effort to score.

The **PAT kicking team** is also brought on the field after a touchdown has been scored. They attempt to score a **point after** (also called the *extra point*). Following a touchdown, the ball is placed on the 2½-yard line. The players line up as they do for a field goal. The kicker is seven yards behind the line of scrimmage. The ball is snapped to the holder; the holder positions and holds the ball for the kicker. The other offensive players again try to block the defensive players from reaching the kicker. If the ball is kicked through the uprights, the offense scores one point.

The following situations may occur when the kicking team is on the field.

1. The *kick is good!* The ball clears the uprights and is kicked between the posts of the upright. Three points are scored in the situation of a field goal, or one point is scored as an *extra point* (after a touchdown).

2. The kick is **blocked.** The defense gets through the offensive line and breaks up the play, stopping the ball from reaching the uprights. The attempt for an extra point or a field goal was thwarted.

3. The snapper or the holder loses control of the ball or fumbles it. Players from both teams go after the ball. The team that recovers the ball gains possession of the ball.

Personal Foul
Roughing the
Kicker

4. The defense causes a penalty by **running into the kicker** or **roughing the kicker.** Because the kicker, with his kicking leg off the ground, is not able to defend himself or respond to oncoming defensive players, he (and the holder) are protected from being tackled. If a defensive player accidentally runs into the kicker or makes contact with him even in a slight way, a running into the kicker five-yard penalty is called. If the defensive player tackles the kicker, a more serious penalty of fifteen yards and an automatic first down is called. However, a penalty is not called on a **blocked kick** if a

defensive player was moving too fast to avoid making contact with the kicker.

5. A fake PAT (point after) may also occur. The kicking team acts as though a kick for a point after will be made, but instead, it attempts to run or pass the ball into the end zone for a **two-point conversion play.** This two-point play is harder to make than the one extra point, but the two-point conversion will be attempted when the game is close, and the difference of a few points might determine the winner.

The two-point conversion play is not always faked. Instead of the kicker coming onto the field to kick an extra point, the quarterback comes on the field to take a snap from the center and attempt a two-point conversion play. The ball has to be moved about two yards in order to cross into the end zone to score the two points. Those two yards are extremely hard to make because of the mass of defensive players positioned to create a human wall. The quarterback may try to hand the ball off to an offensive player whom he believes has the best chance to run with the ball into the end zone. This player may take the "lower path" through the bottom of the wall of players, or he may take a flying leap up over the mound of bodies. The quarterback may pass the ball to a receiver already in the end zone and prepared for the ball. On other occasions, the quarterback may keep the ball and try to get into the end zone himself to score.

Have you ever tried a comical stunt such as seeing how many people can squeeze into a telephone booth or a Volkswagen Bug? Well, a similar feat often occurs when teams go for a two-point conversion by trying to run the ball straight up the middle and across the goal line. Offensive players push and shove to try to make the tiniest space for the ball carrier to squirm through while defensive players push and shove to block those tiny holes. The result? A mound of bodies, player upon player, stacked on top of each other. Sometimes the ball carrier miraculously wriggles through the heap; other times he is pinned to the ground with no possible way to move an inch of his body. It's quite a scene! This pileup must approach record levels for the greatest number of pounds of human mass per square yard.

In summary, the field goal/PAT team can score one, two, or three points. The following reference chart summarizes the points that can be scored by the field goal and the PAT special teams:

TYPE OF OFFENSIVE PLAY	POINTS	WHEN
Field Goal	3	When the offense is within thirty to thirty-five yards of the end zone on a fourth down, or only a few seconds remain on the clock at the end of the first half or the end of the game, instead of trying for a touchdown, an attempt will be made to kick a field goal.
Point After (extra point)	1	After a touchdown, the special teams line up. The ball is placed on the 2½-yard line. The offense tries to kick the ball through the uprights for one additional point. Of course, the defense tries to prevent this from happening.
Two-Point Conversion	2	Instead of trying to kick for the extra point after a touchdown, the offense decides to try to run the ball into the end zone or to pass the ball to a receiver in the end zone to score two points. The center snaps the ball to the quarterback for this play. The two-point conversion is more difficult to complete than the kicked PAT (extra point).

F. The PAT Blocking Team

The blocking team is a special defensive team (eleven players) that tries to stop all the action and scoring attempts made by the field goal or the PAT kicking team. Lined up facing the field goal kicking team or the PAT kicking team, this special team tries to prevent three-point field goals or the one extra point after a touchdown.

If the offense attempts a two-point conversion, the blocking team fights to stop the ball carrier from running (or leaping) into the end zone to earn two points. Unless the blocking team actually sees a play set up for a two-point conversion, they do everything possible to **block the kick** to prevent it from going through the uprights to score. Remember, all this happens in a few short seconds.

That's it, folks! Now you know the basics about the offensive team, the defensive team, and the six special teams. Within the course of a game, many players move on and off the field, fulfill different roles and responsibilities, and perform numerous feats marked by their talent and athleticism. Credit for a great game is often due to the many individuals on the coaching staff who orchestrate all these strategies, coordinate the flow of traffic onto and off of the field, and keep the channels of communication open and working.

6
COMMON
PENALTIES

Football is a game with lots and lots of rules and a mind-boggling number of penalties. It seems for every action there is a corresponding penalty waiting to be imposed, if the play is not performed correctly. You might ask yourself who in the world ever came up with all these rules and penalties! However, the more you watch football, the more familiar you become with the variety and the nuances of these rules. This book is not designed to tell you "everything there is to know about football." This book focuses on the basics; the basics provide you with enough information to understand, appreciate, and enjoy the game. Players, as would be expected, go well beyond these basics and into much more complex rules, plays, strategies, and more precise understanding of different kinds of penalties.

Since few women actually get suited up to play football, it is unlikely that you are a player or need to learn the many nuances of rules and penalties. However, that may change in the very near future! More women may choose careers that place them on the sidelines and require them to understand the nuances of football. Some girls on the high school level already are joining football teams, often as kickers. In the future, this book may need to be revised to include both genders when references are made to players. Only time will tell how many women will infiltrate the game of football and make a home on the playing field.

A. Common Terms

Before we examine a list of common penalties, you will want to become familiar with five common terms that are used in many penalty calls. Each of these terms is used frequently throughout a game.

Loss of down: A loss of a down occurs for a variety of infractions. The down that resulted in a penalty is counted as one of the four downs and may not be repeated. No yardage is made on the play and in fact, the team may be penalized yardage. (See the Penalties Chart.) A loss of a down may occur in these situations:

- A forward pass is thrown when the quarterback was beyond the line of scrimmage;

- An intentional grounding of the ball was done by the quarterback, usually to avoid being sacked;

- A forward pass goes out of bounds;

- A forward pass is touched/caught by an ineligible receiver behind the line of scrimmage.

Loss of Down

Repeat the down: A penalty is enforced but the play and the down are repeated. The ball may be moved back five yards before the down is repeated. A down is often repeated when there is a false start penalty against an offensive lineman.

Automatic first down: The offense is given a first down. Regardless of which down the team was on at the time of the defensive infraction, the team is awarded a new first down. The team will begin a new set of four downs to move the ball ten yards. The most common defensive violations that cause an automatic first down to occur are:

- illegal use of hands, or defensive holding;

- an intentional face mask;

- roughing the kicker;

- roughing the passer;

- pass interference.

Face
Mask

Penalty declined: The team that did not receive the penalty has the option to decline enforcing the penalty against the other team. This is done when the team is in a better position without the enforcement of the penalty.

Penalty
Declined

Offsetting penalties: Both offense and defense had a penalty for the same number of yards. Therefore, the penalties cancel each other out.

Somehow kids are capable of picking up a football and playing an informal game of flag or touch football without getting bogged down with all these rules. The more organized the game becomes with the participation of numerous coaches, players, and referees, the more laden the game becomes with rules and penalties. Interestingly, the rules and the penalties have developed over the years to make football a game that is fair to both teams. Perhaps even more important, many of the rules and the penalties were developed to protect the players, to reduce plays that could more readily lead to injuries. However, I also suspect that some of the complex rules and penalties are designed to make intricate details even more complex, mastery a little more elusive, and the strategies a little more challenging for analytical minds! Is this simply a "male thing?"

B. Common Penalties

I certainly would not recommend that you spend too much of your valuable time memorizing the following chart of common penalties. The chart is included as a quick reference guide. As you watch a game and hear a penalty, you can quickly glance at the chart to get the gist of the call. As the season progresses, you'll find yourself needing to refer to the chart less frequently.

C O M M O N P E N A L T I E S		
Penalty	**Results in**	**Brief Explanation**
Clipping	15 yards	An offensive player blocks a defensive player from the back, where he can't see the offensive player coming.
Defensive Holding	5 yards Automatic first down	While blocking an offensive player who does not have the ball, the defensive player uses his hands to hold an offensive player.

Penalty	Results in	Brief Explanation
Defensive Pass Interference	10 yards Automatic first down at the spot of the foul (College and high school: 15 yard penalty and an automatic first down.)	The defensive player, who is not going after the ball himself, does not give the receiver fair opportunity to catch the ball. There is no interference if the defensive player is looking at the ball and tries to receive or intercept the ball himself.
Delay of Game	5 yards Repeat the down.	The ball is not put into play within the necessary time limit, too many timeouts are taken, or an illegal player substitution occurs.
Encroachment	5 yards	An offensive player (usually a lineman) moves into the neutral zone and makes contact with a defensive player before the ball is snapped or kicked.

Penalty	Results in	Brief Explanation
Fair Catch Interference	15 yards from the spot of the foul.	A player on the kicking team doesn't give the punt returner or kick returner a fair opportunity to catch the ball.
False Start	5 yards Repeat the down.	An offensive lineman takes his three-point stance and then moves before the snap of the ball, or an offensive player makes an abrupt movement to try to draw a defensive player offsides.
Holding	5 or 10 yards	A player holds onto another player or his jersey in order to prevent him from making a play. See offensive holding and defensive holding.

Penalty	Results in	Brief Explanation
Illegal Formation	5 yards	The required seven offensive players are not on the line of scrimmage when the ball is snapped. Illegal formation also occurs when offensive players behind the line of scrimmage are not positioned at least one yard behind the line of scrimmage.
Illegal Forward Pass	5 yards from the point of the foul and loss of the down	The quarterback goes past the line of scrimmage and then throws the ball. (The ball must be released behind the line of scrimmage.)

Penalty	Results in	Brief Explanation
Illegal Motion	5 yards	An offensive player in motion runs toward the line of scrimmage (instead of parallel to the line of scrimmage or away from the line of scrimmage), or a running back starts on the line of scrimmage but then moves back off the line of scrimmage before the ball is snapped.
Illegal Procedure	5 yards	This call refers to several illegal offensive procedures, including *false start*, *illegal formation*, and *illegal shift*.
Illegal Shift	5 yards	More than one offensive player shifts positions before the ball is snapped.

Penalty	Results in	Brief Explanation
Ineligible Receiver Downfield	10 yards	An offensive lineman (tackle, guard, or center) who is not eligible to catch the ball and who did not make contact with a defensive player moves down the field before a pass is thrown.
Ineligible Player Downfield	5 yards	An ineligible player on the kicking team runs down the field too soon before the ball is kicked.
Incidental Face Mask	5 yards	A player grabs the face mask of an opponent but immediately lets go. The grab on the face mask was not deliberate or intentional.
Intentional Face Mask	15 yards or, if in the red zone, half the distance to the goal line.	A player grabs an opponent's face mask and yanks, pulls, or twists the face mask to the degree that the player's head is turned. This is a personal foul.

Penalty	Results in	Brief Explanation
Intentional Grounding	10 yards Loss of the down	The quarterback throws the ball toward the ground in an area where there is no eligible receiver. The ball is thrown to avoid a sack or a loss of yards.
Neutral Zone Infraction	5 yards	A defensive player moves beyond the neutral zone before the ball is snapped.
Offensive Holding	10 yards	An offensive player holds a defensive player, usually to keep the defensive player from tackling the ball carrier or the quarterback.
Offensive Pass Interference	10 yards	An offensive player tries to prevent the defensive player from catching the ball (making an interception) by pushing or holding onto him.

Penalty	Results in	Brief Explanation
Offside	5 yards Repeat the down	A player positions himself with part of his body over the line of scrimmage or moves too soon across the line of scrimmage.
Pass Interference	10 yards	A player is not given an opportunity to catch a pass. See offensive pass interference and defensive pass interference.
Personal Foul	15 yards	Personal fouls are called for several infractions: unnecessary roughness, roughing the kicker, roughing the passer, clipping, piling on, etc.
Piling On	15 yards Automatic first down	A player piles on top of the ball carrier after the whistle is blown and the play has ended. Often the intent is to hurt the ball carrier.

Penalty	Results in	Brief Explanation
Roughing the Kicker/Punter	15 yards Automatic first down	A defensive player who has not touched the ball forcefully runs into or tackles the punter after the ball is kicked. Contact with the kicker is legal if the kick is blocked, and the defensive player cannot stop his forward momentum.
Roughing the Passer	15 yards Automatic first down	A defensive player makes rough contact with or tackles the quarterback after the ball has been released.
Running into the Kicker/Punter	5 yards	A defensive player runs into the kicker or punter unintentionally. Contact occurs because the forward momentum cannot be stopped in time. This foul is not as severe as roughing the passer, which is considered intentional.

Penalty	Results in	Brief Explanation
Spearing	15 yards	One player hits another player with his helmet in an attempt to injure the other player.
Unsportsman-like Conduct	15 yards	A player shows unsportsmanlike conduct. This includes abusive language and gestures, taunting players on the other team, or making contact with an official.

Another way of categorizing penalties is by grouping them according to the number of yards involved. If the penalty is called on the defense, the offense is awarded with extra yardage. If the penalty is called on the offense, the offense loses yardage. Another way to look at this is to realize that the five-yard penalties are not as severe or as grave an infraction as the fifteen-yard penalties.

5-Yard Penalties	10-Yard Penalties	15-Yard Penalties
defensive holding	defensive pass interference	clipping
delay of game	ineligible receiver downfield	fair catch interference
encroachment	intentional grounding	intentional face mask
false start	offensive holding	personal foul
illegal formation	offensive pass interference	piling on
illegal forward pass		roughing the kicker/punter
illegal motion		roughing the passer
illegal procedure		spearing
illegal shift		unsportsmanlike conduct
ineligible player downfield		
incidental face mask		
neutral zone infraction		
offside		
running into the kicker/punter		

7
TIPS AND FINAL THOUGHTS

Now that you have a strong foundation of the basics of football, I hope you are ready and eager to kick back in your comfortable chair and enjoy a game or two. You may want to keep *Mom's Pocket Guide to Watching Football* by your side and look up some of the terms that you hear as you watch the game. Don't be surprised when others enjoying the game with you reach for the book!

Tips for Stadium Fans:

In case you are heading out to a stadium to see a game in person, here are a few suggestions for those of you who have not attended many games in the past.

1. Dress appropriately and in layers. Games can be downright miserable if you are roasting, freezing, and risking frostbite, or drenched in a downpour. If there is a remote chance of inclement weather, bring rain gear (or large plastic garbage bags), a warm jacket, hat, and gloves. Wear comfortable shoes or warm boots.

2. If you are so fortunate to be going to an outdoor game on a nice, sunny day, bring sunscreen. You may also want a hat, sunglasses, and a bottle of water.

3. Some stadiums have hard wooden or metal benches. A

blanket or a cushion to sit on may make the hours of sitting more comfortable. A stadium chair with a back that clips onto flat benches is not a bad idea if you prefer to have a little back support.

4. Bring binoculars! Even with big projection screens in some stadiums, binoculars are great if your seat is not located down close to the field. Even with good seating, binoculars give you a much more interesting view of players on and off the field!

5. Leave the cell phone at home! This is one nice way not to annoy other fans near you.

Tips for Moms with High School Players:

On more than one occasion people would ask me, "How can you let your son play football?" My response was, "How could I prevent him from playing football?" Of course, many parenting strategies could have been applied to prevent him from participating, but when you have an athletic son (or daughter) who has always been involved in sports, few reasons justify barring him (or her) from playing. From their passionate participation, they learn many skills, and they dare to dream. So, if your son has a serious desire to play football and wishes to commit himself to the sport, I believe the role of the parent is to offer support. Here are a few tips that I would like to share with "moms."

1. Support your son's decision to play and don't hesitate to discuss the importance of keeping the balance between football and schoolwork. A commitment to both is necessary. Both place demands on his time and energy.

2. Do not burden your son with your worries or fears about injuries. While you may often have this on your mind, avoid giving "energy" to that kind of thinking. Players do not need to be reminded of possible injuries.

3. Focus more on doing what you can do to assure that your son has good nutrition to build a strong, healthy body. Returning to the four basic food groups and refueling with lots of fruits and vegetables in between meals works for many growing bodies.

4. Recognize the importance of your son's workouts. If he is committed to working out and is dedicated to his routine conditioning, try to respect his routine and give him the time and the space to do what he feels he needs to do without any unnecessary nagging or making him feel guilty about the time he spends working out. Get used to the fact that meals and other family activities may rotate around his schedule.

5. Figure out how much space he wants. Some players like to have their parents hanging around before games, after games, at practices, etc. Others find a little more distance and separation work better. Listen to what your son prefers and voice your preference. See if a comfortable agreement can be reached.

6. Stay off the field! It's hard, and there may be times you want to run to his side, but don't. The coaches and the trainers are there, and your son knows you are there "in total spirit."

7. Be sensitive to your son's feelings after a loss. Your son and his teammates were the ones who put their will and energy into winning. Many times your son may feel disheartened about the loss for much more personal reasons. Don't harp on him. Don't gripe about the refs or the calls. Don't go overboard in exhibiting or expressing your disappointment. Sometimes it's best to give a hug and be quiet.

8. Praise and congratulate your son on the things he did well or things the team did well during the course of the

game. Pushing, pushing, pushing to perform better, better, better can destroy a player's love of the game. I've seen competitive parents ruin the joy of the game for their sons on several occasions. Praise and positive feedback bring much better results than criticism and degrading comments. Let him have fun! It's his time, his glory, and his passion for the game. Let him enjoy it.

Tips for Moms Whose Sons Move to Higher Levels

If your son is recruited in his senior year of high school for a college scholarship, the following tips may assist you with the process.

1. Work together with your son to determine the best way to handle the process. The high school coaches can explain the recruiting process, the rules, and the guidelines. Handbooks that explain the process to parents and players are also available. Take the time to read the information and be sure you understand the rules. Violations of the rules can affect your son's scholarship opportunities.

2. At some point, you may need to step in to screen calls; otherwise, your son may find himself overwhelmed and annoyed by excessive calls from coaches and recruiters. Consider limiting recruiting calls to a specific time period and on specific days of the week. If they are interested in your son, they'll call back.

3. Help your son by organizing a filing system for the letters and brochures he will receive from various colleges and universities. This information may help him later if he wants to select campuses to visit prior to announcing his intent to enroll in a specific college or university.

4. Your son will be asked to complete a variety of questionnaires that ask about his football history, stats, phys-

ical characteristics, and more. Take the time to gather the information and compile a page with the pertinent information. Keep this in your filing system so you have the information available at your fingertips.

Many players know their football years will end at the end of their college careers. They will forever look back on those years with special memories. A relatively small number of college players will have the opportunity to move to the highest level of football, the NFL. The following tips may help you if your son aspires to entering the NFL draft or to seeking a position as a free agent.

1. Instead of receiving calls from NFL coaches, the parents and the players will receive calls and packets of information from sports agents. Some agents are a part of large sports agencies and others work independently. Some have polished promotional brochures, and some use basic introductory letters. Players are not allowed to make any written or verbal commitments to agents until the end of their college season. Players are not allowed to receive any gifts, incentives, or even a dinner or soft drink from an agent; to do so threatens their eligibility status.

2. Selecting the right agent will be an important decision for your son. He will want to select an agent he feels comfortable with and trusts.

3. Your son's coaches and athletic department can provide you with information about agents. Some schools offer workshops for parents and players to discuss the process of selecting an agent. Players often confer with former teammates who are in the NFL to learn more about their agents, including their satisfaction with their agent's ability to negotiate contracts and to provide the desired level of services.

Tips for Players from Kailee

Kailee can be succinct. Here are the tips he would like to pass on to players.

1. Have fun during conditioning, practices, and games.

2. Try hard...play hard. Give your best in every game.

3. Don't neglect the books. Education is important. You will need it to advance to the next level, and you will need and benefit from the education after your football career ends.

4. Make wise decisions. Think before you act, and take time to make wise decisions that are right for you. For every action, there's a reaction. Sometimes the reactions bring unfavorable consequences that will affect your opportunities.

5. Think for yourself. Don't be afraid to make your own decisions.

Give Credit Where Credit is Due

Student-athletes are to be greatly admired. Too few people realize the amount of commitment players must have if they are to succeed on the field and in the classroom. Gone are the days when a player could be a great athlete but not also be required to meet serious academic standards. The demands on student-athletes' time, bodies, and minds are intense. They need to discover sophisticated ways to balance all three. Student-athletes deserve resounding applause and praise for their dedication and commitment to training and performing mentally as well as physically.

There's great value in recognizing that people have different abilities and kinds of intelligences. Some are strong verbally, some are strong mathematically, and some are strong musically. Athletes are strong kinesthetically. Kinesthetically-gifted individuals are blessed with the ability to adjust their physical performance to carry out specific tasks. They have an acute sense of timing, balance, dexterity, flexibility, strength, and speed that go beyond an average person's physical abilities. Their often superb coordination skills are exhibited in body movements that are impossible without a special kind of body rhythm and fitness. If a player is seen as having "more brawn than brain," let's upgrade the value of brawn, for it in itself is a form of athletic intelligence that is not readily acquired.

One myth that is well worth debunking is that football players are "thugs," poor role models, or overly aggressive individuals even when they are off the field. Unfortunately, the media seems to focus on the negative behaviors of a few players. This leaves the image in people's minds that the majority of football players come from that same mold, and yet there are hundreds and hundreds of stories to be told about football players who are active members in their communities. They donate time and money to local charities, organizations, and programs. Many professional athletes spend part of their days off involved in community service. Many professional players establish foundations to grant scholarships or create programs that help others. The "attitude of gratitude" is much more prevalent than the media would lead one to believe. It's sad that attention and recognition are not given to the hundreds of players who are positive role models. The majority of the players have very large hearts, very sharing spirits, and they make excellent role models for our youth. They deserve much more positive recognition than they generally receive.

Be Comfortable with How Much You Know

Avoid feeling like you need to understand every aspect of football before you can enjoy a good football game! I'll be honest. I know enough of the basics to enjoy the game, but I could *never* play the game myself, and I could *never* coach even the first year of peewee football or flag football. That's okay because I have no desire to know *that* much. I smile when true football fanatics speak the technical jargon, sprinkling conversations with their knowledge of complex playbook diagrams, or intentionally trying "one-upmanship" in their choice of words. I am happy with what I know, but I am always willing to learn a little more. I hope that by now you are more comfortable and can have a similar attitude. Without a doubt, understanding football is an ongoing process. You will never reach the point where you "know it all"—neither will players or coaches.

How far will you take your newly-acquired football fanaticism? Perhaps you will follow in the footsteps of my sister Kathryn. Kathryn has acquired more than enough information to understand the game. When I asked her to describe her newfound love for the game, she responded:

"Five years have now passed since my 'awakening.' I now carry a portable TV with me that I can plug into my car lighter if in fact I have to work on a game day. I pull over to the side of the road, park, and watch as many minutes as I can on my breaks. However, I now make every attempt possible to create a work schedule that gives me every Sunday off during football season. The Stanford T-shirts, pictures, and decals are stored away. Now my car is plastered with Vikings decals, bumper stickers, magnets, and license plate holders. During the season, I wear Vikings pins and earrings to work where I already have a carved Vikings bookend, posters, and pennants. The NFL schedule is prominently displayed above my desk. I check eight different football websites on a regular basis, but I only get one football publication, *The Viking Update*. I wear my purple Vikings sweatshirt and jacket. Do you know how few outfits coordinate with that purple? When the Vikings lose, I always wear black to work and everyone knows not to mess with me! My partner has a collection of more than 100 hats, but now he only chooses from his Vikings stash. *Ha!* Who would have imagined that I would be this much of a football fanatic?"

I, for one, would never have imagined this transformation. She has far surpassed me with her fanaticism and rahrah! Ahhh, but I have it all in my heart. May your heart also be filled with yelling-good times, fond memories, and an endless supply of *rahrah!*

GLOSSARY OF COMMON TERMS

Another way to learn more and more about the game is to listen to the announcers and then to look up unfamiliar terms in the following glossary. Football talk can easily sound like a foreign language to people who have not been around the game much or who have not had the opportunity to learn the basics. For two years, I watched two or three games a week and compiled lists and lists of terms that I heard announcers use. The result is the following glossary of terms. Of course, Kailee, the co-author of this book, then got to work to provide the definitions. Needless to say, in the entire process, I learned a lot!

assists   Two defensive players tackle the ball carrier at the same time.

audibles   After seeing how the defense is lined up, the quarterback calls out a different play to his offense while at the line of scrimmage. Audibles allow the quarterback to adjust the play in response to the defensive formation that forms on the field.

automatic first down   In addition to moving the ball ahead five, ten, or fifteen yards depending on the penalty, the offense is given a new set of four downs to move the ball ten yards. Automatic first downs are given for a variety of penalties, including personal foul, defensive holding, roughing the kicker, or roughing the passer.

ball is dead   The play is over.

blitz   One or more extra defensive players, either linebackers or defensive backs, who would normally drop back to cover action deep in the field, fly up to the line of scrimmage to disrupt or sack the quarterback. Instead of the usual four defensive players that rush the quarterback, there are at least five defensive players going for the quarterback in a blitz.

blocked kick (blocked punt)   On a punt, an attempted field goal kick, or a kick for a point after a touchdown, a defensive player breaks through the line of scrimmage and blocks the kick.

blocking (blockers)   The body is used in blocking to keep other players from going where they want to go. Ideally, to block is to stop. Players can use their hands to push the player out of the way, but they can't grab. If they grab another player, they are called for *holding*. Both offensive players and defensive players block their opponents. Offensive players block to protect the quarterback from incoming defensive players, and they block to create a "hole" through which the ball carrier runs. Defensive players block to prevent the offensive play from developing.

blown coverage   A defensive player did not provide the coverage he was assigned, so an offensive play was made.

bomb   A bomb is a long pass thrown by the quarterback to a receiver far downfield.

bump and run   A defensive back, usually a cornerback, bumps or pushes a receiver in an attempt to throw off his timing or change his route so he is not in position for a pass. The bump has to occur before the receiver is five yards past the line of scrimmage, or there will be a penalty.

carries   Carries refers to the number of times a player runs with the ball (carries the ball) in a game.

center   This offensive lineman in the center of the line of scrimmage snaps the ball between his legs to the quarterback.

clipping   A clipping penalty is caused when an offensive player illegally blocks a defensive player from the back. This rule is designed to help protect the safety of the players.

completion   This is also referred to as *pass completion*. An eligible receiver catches a forward pass. In the NFL, the receiver must have both feet in bounds when he catches, and he must have the ball under control. In high school and college, only one foot needs to be in bounds.

converting a third down   If the play on the third down results in sufficient yards to make a new first down, the third down has been *converted to a first down*. Converting a third down indicates that the offense is doing its job in moving the ball forward. If the down is not converted, the offense must make sufficient yardage on the fourth down in order to keep the ball. If the offense is not confident that the required yards can be gained on the fourth down, they will punt the ball to the other team.

corner kick   The punter kicks the ball toward the end zone but out of bounds on the corner of the field. The offense takes over at the point the ball goes out of bounds.

cornerback   The cornerback is a defensive back who plays in the back of the field and in the corner. The cornerback usually covers the wide receivers on pass plays. Cornerbacks are part of the secondary.

dead ball   This term is used to signal that the play is over. The ball is no longer in play.

defense   The defense is the team without the ball. They defend their half of the field to try to keep the offense from coming into their territory and scoring in their end zone.

defensive backs   Defensive backs are players who are "back" behind the line of scrimmage and in the "back" of the field. They are also called the *secondary. Cornerbacks, safeties,* and *nickel* or *dime backs* are defensive backs.

defensive ends   The defensive ends are defensive linemen who position themselves on the "end" of the defensive line, which is on the line of scrimmage.

defensive linemen   The defensive linemen are the players lined up on the line of scrimmage. They usually are the defensive tackles and the defensive ends.

defensive tackles   These are the defensive linemen who are positioned on the line of scrimmage where they face the offensive guards and the center.

deflecting the ball   The ball is tipped or knocked off its course when a defensive player jumps up in the air, waves his arms and manages to make contact with the ball when it is in the air. The goal is to force an *incomplete pass* and possibly even a *turnover,* which is also called an *interception.*

delay of game   In most situations, the quarterback has forty seconds to get the play started. The clock starts when the ball is placed on the line of scrimmage. A five yard penalty is given if the offense exceeds its forty-second time cap. The down is repeated.

dime back   A dime back is a sixth defensive player put in the secondary to cover plays that will likely involve passing.

double foul   A foul is called on both teams. Both fouls have equal penalties, so the fouls offset each other.

double team   Two players cover one opposing player who is considered to be a threat in an attempt to "shut out" the talented player. Usually double teaming involves two defensive players covering one offensive player such as a receiver. However, two offensive linemen may also double team a powerful defensive player.

down the ball   The player with the ball puts his knee down on the ground to signal the end of the play.

downs   Downs are attempts to move the ball forward. The offense gets four downs to move the ball a total of ten yards. Once the ten yards is reached, a new set of downs is given to the offense.

draw play   The quarterback drops back to give the impression that he is going to pass, but instead of passing, he hands the ball off to a running back. This offensive play is an attempt to confuse or disrupt the defense.

drawing a player offsides   An offensive lineman or the quarterback tries to trick a defensive player into jumping across the line of scrimmage before the ball is snapped. Even though the offense must remain stationary until the ball is snapped, an offensive player tries to cause a defensive reaction that will lead to a penalty. If the slight movement is seen by the refs, the offense receives the offsides penalty.

drop back   The player moves farther back from the line of scrimmage. For example, a quarterback may drop back further in the pocket to throw. A punt returner may drop back further in the field to receive a punt, etc.

dropped snap   The center, who snaps the ball between his legs to the quarterback, drops the ball during the snap.

dual possession   On a fumble, an offensive and a defensive player have equal possession of the ball when the fumble is recovered by both players simultaneously. The ball remains with the offense.

encroachment   This five-yard penalty is called when an offensive player moves into the neutral zone and makes contact with a defensive player before the ball is snapped.

end zone   The end zone is the ten-yard area between the goal line and the end line on each end of the field.

extra point   The extra point is the same as PAT (point after touchdown). The PAT kicking team attempts to score one extra point after a touchdown by kicking the ball through the uprights.

face mask   This penalty occurs when an offensive or a defensive player grabs another player's face mask during the act of blocking or tackling. An *intentional face mask* (such as when a defensive player grabs a running back by his face mask to pull him down) is a fifteen-yard penalty. An *incidental* (unintentional) face mask, a five-yard penalty, occurs when a player accidentally grabs or has contact with another player's face mask but quickly lets go.

fair catch   A receiving player on a kick off return team or a punt return team waves his hand in the air above his head to signal to the defensive players that they cannot tackle him because he does not intend to run with the ball. The defense has to give him room to catch the ball. He cannot run after he catches the ball.

false start   This occurs when an offensive lineman takes his stance and then moves before the snap of the ball. Once the player takes his stance, he must remain completely still until the snap. This is a five-yard penalty on the offense and the down is repeated.

field goal   The offense kicks the ball through the uprights for three points. Field goal attempts are made on the fourth down when the offense is too far away for a touchdown or too little time remains on the clock to move the ball through several plays. The center snaps the ball to the holder, who holds the ball for the kicker to kick.

field goal team   The field goal team is the specialized team that comes onto the field for a fourth down. The kicking team attempts to kick a field goal for three points. The field goal blocking team attempts to disrupt the play so the field goal isn't achieved.

first down   The first down is the first play an offensive team has when it gets possession of the ball. The offense has four downs (attempts) to move the ball ten yards. Getting many first downs in a game indicates the offense is moving the ball well.

flags   Flags are used by the referees and officials to indicate a penalty or infraction has occurred.

flanker   A flanker is the name used for a wide receiver who has lined up behind the line of scrimmage.

4–3 defense   This is a defensive formation that places four defensive linemen on the line of scrimmage and three linebackers behind the line of scrimmage.

foul   Any offensive or defensive infraction or violation that results in a penalty is called a foul.

fourth down   The fourth down is the last attempt for the offense to move the ball the complete ten yards necessary to get a new first down.

formation   The term formation refers to the offensive or defensive arrangement or alignment of players on the field for a specific kind of play.

free safety The free safety is a player in the secondary. He is the last defensive player in the backfield. If the ball carrier gets past the free safety, a touchdown is likely.

fullback A fullback is a running back who is an eligible ball carrier but more often blocks to help clear a running path for another running back.

fumble A fumble occurs any time a player has possession of the ball and loses it. The ball can be recovered by players from either team.

goal line The goal line is the zero-yard line. A *touchdown* is scored when the ball is carried over the goal line or is caught past the goal line in the end zone.

"ground can't cause a fumble" This expression refers to the rule that states that the ground cannot be the cause of a fumble. If the ball carrier hits the ground and the ball pops out of his hold because it hits the ground, it is not considered a fumble.

guards The guards are offensive linemen positioned on the line of scrimmage on each side of the center. Guards are mainly blockers and are not eligible to receive the ball.

Hail Mary A "Hail Mary" is a long pass that is "all or nothing." It is the last attempt to score a touchdown before the first half or the very end of the game.

halfback The halfback is a fast running back whose main job is to get the ball from the quarterback and run as far downfield as possible. The halfback is also called a tailback.

hand-off The quarterback hands the ball off to a running back. It some cases, the ball is handed off to a wide receiver. Hand-offs are used only for running plays, not passing plays.

hang in the pocket This occurs when the quarterback stays inside the protected area the linemen have created for him (pocket) before passing the ball.

hang time The length of time a punt is in the air is called the hang time. A long and high punt with long hang time gives the players extra time to get down the field to tackle the punt receiver.

hash marks   The hash marks are the short lines in the middle part of the field that mark every yard. The ball is marked or "spotted" on the closest hash mark.

holder   The holder is the offensive player who has the ball snapped to him so he can hold the ball in position for the field goal kicker.

holding   Holding occurs when a player tries to hold onto the arm, jersey, or any part of an opposing player's body in order to keep the player from moving or making a play. Holding results in a ten-yard penalty when an offensive player uses his hands to grab and hold onto a defensive player while blocking. Defensive players can also be called for holding if they hold an offensive player who is not the ball carrier.

huddle   The huddle is the place where all the players "get on the same page" and make sure they know what they are supposed to do for the next play. In the offensive huddle, the quarterback calls the play and reveals the count that will be used so players know when the ball will be snapped. In the defensive huddle, the middle linebacker gives the defensive formation that will be used. The calls are given in a coded language that can consist of color words, numbers, and letters.

hurry-up offense   A hurry-up offense is used in the *two minute drill,* the last two minutes of a half. The hurry-up offense involves passes to a receiver who runs out of bounds as quickly as possible after catching the pass. This stops the clock.

I-Formation   The I-Formation is an offensive setup where the center, the quarterback, the fullback, and the halfback are lined up behind each other.

illegal formation   This is a five-yard penalty that happens when the offensive line does not have a legal formation of seven men on the line of scrimmage.

illegal motion   Illegal motion occurs when an offensive player in motion runs toward the line of scrimmage, or a running back starts on the line of scrimmage but moves off the line of scrimmage before the snap. This penalty is also called if more than one offensive player is in motion. This is a five-yard penalty.

illegal player downfield   An offensive lineman, who is designated for blocking, cannot go downfield for a pass. If he goes downfield, he is ruled as an *illegal player downfield*. A five-yard penalty is called on the offense.

illegal procedure   This is a general term for several kinds of illegal offensive procedures such as a false start, illegal formation, or an illegal shift.

illegal shift   This penalty occurs when more than one offensive player shifts positions before the ball is snapped.

incomplete pass (incompletion)   The pass was not completed.

ineligible receiver   A tackle, guard, or center who did not make contact with a defensive player moves down the field before the pass is thrown. These players are not eligible receivers, nor are they permitted to go downfield.

instant replay   Activated in the 1999 professional football season, each team can request that a play be reviewed (challenged) on three occasions in each half of the game. If the call that was made on the field is upheld by the instant replay, the team that requested the instant replay is charged with one timeout. If the call on the field is reversed after reviewing the play, a timeout is not charged. Instant replays cannot be requested by either team in the last two minutes of a game.

intended receiver   The receiver to whom the quarterback intended to throw the ball on a pass play is called the intended receiver.

intentional grounding   A ten-yard penalty with a loss of the down is called when a quarterback throws a pass to an area of the field where no receiver has a realistic chance of reaching the ball. The quarterback throws the ball to the ground when he is under defensive pressure and wants to avoid a sack.

interception   A defensive player catches (intercepts) a pass intended for an offensive player. This causes a turnover.

The play continues until the player with the ball is tackled, run out of bounds, or scores a touchdown.

kick off (kick off team, kick off return team)   At the beginning of each half and after a team scores a touchdown and attempts a PAT, special teams come on the field to kick the ball far down the field. A kick off is a transition play in which the possession of the ball transfers from one team (the kick off team) to the other team (the kick off return team).

lateral pass   This is a sideways pass that one offensive player throws to another. Since the pass is going sideways instead of forward, it can occur beyond the line of scrimmage.

line of scrimmage   This invisible line passes through each end of the football when the football is placed on the field prior to the beginning of a play.

linebackers   These defensive players are behind the line of scrimmage and positioned behind the defensive line. There can be outside, middle, and inside linebackers.

linemen   Linemen are offensive and defensive players who are lined up on the line of scrimmage at the beginning of a play.

live ball   When a whistle is not blown to end a play, a ball that is loose as a result of a fumble can be recovered by either team.

loss of down   A loss of down occurs with specific penalties. Though no yards are gained, the down still counts as one of the offense's four downs and cannot be redone.

man-to-man coverage   This strategy is used during a pass play, where each possible receiver is covered by a specific defensive player. The defensive player stays close to the receiver to try to tackle him if he gets the ball. More simply, he wants to keep the receiver from making a play.

man in motion   This expression refers to an eligible receiver who runs parallel to the line of scrimmage before the ball is snapped. Only one man may be in motion.

middle linebacker   The middle linebacker is a linebacker who is in "back of" or behind the line of scrimmage and positioned in the middle of the field. He is often nicknamed "Mike."

muffed ball   A returner makes contact with the ball when he tries to catch it, but is unable to hold on to the ball (control the ball). This is different from a fumble because a fumble occurs when the player loses possession of a ball after he had the ball under his control.

neutral zone   The neutral zone is the area between the two lines of scrimmage. It's the length of the football.

neutral zone infraction   A five-yard penalty that occurs when a defensive player on the line of scrimmage moves into the neutral zone before the ball is snapped.

nickel back   The term "nickel" is used when a fifth defensive back is added to the secondary (back field) in a passing situation (nickel defense). Usually there are just four defensive backs (two cornerbacks, a strong safety, and a free safety).

nose tackle   The nose tackle is the defensive tackle who is lined up directly across from the center.

offensive line   The seven offensive players who are lined up on the line of scrimmage are called the offensive line. The offensive line includes the tackles, guards, center, tight end, and a wide receiver. Seven offensive players must be on the line of scrimmage when the ball is snapped.

offside   This five-yard penalty and repeat of the down is called any time a player has any part of his body across the line of scrimmage (in the neutral zone) before the ball is snapped.

off-setting penalties   Both teams receive a penalty of equal distance, canceling each other.

onside kick   This intentionally short kick is used toward the end of the game when the kicking team is losing. The kicker intentionally kicks the ball short (but it must go at least ten yards) with hopes that his team will be able to recover the ball.

outside linebacker   This defensive player is in "back of" or behind the defensive line and on the outside part of the field.

passing lane (pass route)   The passing lane or pass route is the path through which the receiver intends to run before he is thrown the ball. Offensive players try to block the defense to help make the passing lane open for the receiver.

pass interference   A receiver must be given a chance to catch a pass. A defensive pass interference penalty is called when a defensive player knocks the wide receiver off his route so that he doesn't keep the ball. In college, the receiver cannot be hit when the ball is in the air. In the NFL, the receiver cannot be hit after he is five yards past the line of scrimmage. An offensive pass interference is called if the receiver pushes or holds onto the defensive player to prevent him from making an interception.

pass rushing   Defensive linemen put pressure on the quarterback when he drops back to pass. They try to force the quarterback to pass quickly, or they attempt to sack him.

passing yards   These are statistics that indicate the number of yards the quarterback completed by passing to receivers in a game.

PAT kicking team   This is the point-after-touchdown special kicking team that comes onto the field to attempt to kick a point after a touchdown. This is also the team that usually attempts field goal kicks.

penalty refused/declined   A team can refuse or accept a penalty imposed on the other team, depending upon which is to their advantage. For example, if the offense just scored a touchdown, but the defense was penalized five yards, the offense would want to keep the touchdown and decline the penalty against the defense.

personal foul   This is a general term used for infractions that involve a fifteen-yard penalty. Personal fouls can include spearing, intentional face mask, dirty play (tripping), roughing the kicker or the passer, and unsportsmanlike conduct.

picked off   The ball was intercepted or taken away by the other team.

pitch   The quarterback receives the ball, but instead of handing it (hand to hand) to a running back, he pitches (tosses it) it to the running back. A pitch cannot be a forward pass.

place kicker   This is the kicker who places the ball on a tee for a kick off.

play-action-pass   This is an offensive play in which the quarterback fakes a handoff and then throws a pass.

pocket   The pocket is an area formed around the quarterback by the offensive linemen who try to protect the quarterback long enough for him to throw a pass.

point after   This is the one extra point that the PAT special team tries to kick after a touchdown has been scored.

possession   A team with possession is the team that has the ball.

pump fake   The quarterback tries to fool the defense by pretending to pass to a specific receiver, but he does not release the ball. He pulls the ball back (pumps) and throws the ball in a different direction and to a different receiver.

punt (punter)   A punt is the kick (or kicker) of the ball down the field on a fourth down, which turns the ball over to the other team.

punting team   This is the eleven-man special transition team that comes onto the field in the fourth down. The ball is snapped to the punter who kicks the ball as far downfield as possible.

punt return team   This is the eleven-man special transition team that comes onto the field in the fourth down to receive the ball and move the ball as far downfield as possible.

quarterback option   The quarterback keeps the ball and tries to run around the end of the defensive line (usually around the defensive end). From that position, he then has the option of running up the field to gain yardage or throwing a lateral pass (sideways pass) to a running back

quarterback sneak   This is an offensive play in which the quarterback keeps the ball and pushes forward to make short yardage in order to make a first down. The quarterback often runs behind the guard; both push forward or dive to try to get the ball forward enough to make the necessary yards.

receiver   A receiver is an offensive player who is eligible to run down the field and catch a pass.

recover the ball   When the ball is fumbled, the player who gains possession of it recovers the ball.

red zone   The last twenty yards before the end zone is called the red zone. Once the offense reaches the red zone, it is much more likely to score.

repeat the down   The down that was just played didn't count. The offensive team gets to redo the down because of a penalty call. Depending on the penalty, the ball may be moved to a different yard line.

returned kick   The punt returner or the kick returner catches the ball and runs with it until he either goes out of bounds, is tackled, loses his footing, and falls or fumbles.

reverse   This offensive play occurs when the running back gets the ball from the quarterback, runs parallel to the line of scrimmage and hands the ball off to another offensive player (a flanker or a receiver) who is running in the opposite direction. This play attempts to confuse the defense.

roll dead   When the ball is kicked and no punt returner or kick off returner is in the area to catch the ball, the ball rolls to a stop and is then ruled "dead." The next play begins from that spot on the field.

roughing the kicker   A fifteen-yard penalty is called when a defensive player makes contact with the kicker after the ball has been kicked. No penalty is called if the kicker is hit when the kick is blocked and the defensive player could not stop his forward momentum.

roughing the passer   A fifteen-yard penalty is called on the defense when a defensive player hits the quarterback after the ball has been released.

running into the kicker   A five-yard penalty is called when a defensive player accidentally runs into the kicker or has contact with the kicker.

running backs   This is a general term for offensive players who run with the ball. Tailbacks, halfbacks, and fullbacks are different kinds of running backs.

running lane   This is the path the ball carrier intends to run on a specific play.

rushing (rushing yards)   Rushing means running with the ball. Rushing yards are the statistics kept that count the number of yards running backs accumulate in a game and a season.

sack (sacking the quarterback)   The quarterback gets tackled with the ball while he is behind the line of scrimmage. Statistics show the number of sacks the defensive players make per game and the number of sacks individual players accomplish within a given season.

safety (a play)   The quarterback or an offensive player with the ball is tackled in his own end zone. The defense scores two points and the offense loses the ball. After the safety is scored, the ball is taken to the 20-yard line and kicked to the team that earned the two points.

safety (a player)   A safety is a defensive player in the secondary, or the back part of the field. The job of the safeties is to protect the backfield so no offensive player can enter the area and move toward the end zone to score. There are two kinds of safeties: the strong safety and the free safety.

Sam   This is a nickname for a strong outside linebacker, a defensive position.

snap count   This verbal code used on the line of scrimmage lets the offensive players know when the center will snap the ball to begin a play. The snap count is announced in the huddle before the players take their positions on the line of scrimmage and in the backfield.

scramble   The quarterback runs or is forced out of the pocket when no receiver is available for a pass. Instead of losing yardage, the quarterback scrambles forward with the ball to make a few more yards. The quarterback may end the play by sliding forward with his feet first. No defensive player can hit the quarterback when he slides to end a play.

screen   The quarterback drops back and the linemen run downfield to set up a barrier or a screen to protect the ball carrier, who jumps up and catches the ball behind the line of scrimmage.

secondary   The defensive backs (two corners, free safety, and strong safety) are all called the secondary.

shotgun   This is an offensive play in which the quarterback stands in the back of the pocket to throw a long pass.

sidelines   The sidelines are the lines that indicate the boundaries on each side of the field.

snap the ball   This is the quick, continuous motion of the center when he grips the ball and passes it between his legs to the quarterback.

snapper   This is a term used for the player on the PAT kicking team who snaps the ball between his legs to the holder, the player who holds the ball for the kicker.

spearing   Spearing is a personal foul that is called when a player hits another player with his helmet in an attempt to cause injury.

special teams   The six special teams are the groups of players that are sent onto the field for transition plays (where the ball is turned over to the other team) or for the extra point attempts after a touchdown.

split end   This is the name used for a wide receiver who is one of the seven offensive players lined up on the line of scrimmage at the beginning of an offensive play.

spotted   To spot a ball means to place the ball on the field on the yard line where the next play begins. The ball is spotted on the yard line where the play ended.

stiff arm   The ball carrier can use a stiff arm to hold off defensive players or to try to avoid being tackled. This is legal.

strip the ball   A defensive player strips the ball when he pulls the ball from the hands of the offensive ball carrier.

strong safety   This is a defensive player in the back of the field who defends against running and passing plays.

strong side   The strong side of the field is the offensive side that has the tight end.

sweep   This is an offensive play in which blockers try to form a wall against the defense so the ball carrier can run a path that takes him out of bounds and stops the clock.

T-formation   This offensive formation (also called a Split T-Formation) is used when the fullback and the halfback are behind the quarterback but a few yards to the right and the left of the quarterback. The formation forms a "T."

tackled for a loss   The ball carrier is tackled behind the line of scrimmage, so yards are lost on the play.

tackles   A defensive player uses his arms and his body to bring the ball carrier to the ground. Tackles can only be made on the ball carrier. Other kinds of contact on the field are blocks, not tackles.

take a knee   A receiver catches the ball in the end zone and puts one knee on the ground to end the play. This play is ruled a touchback. The ball is then placed on the 20-yard line to begin the next play.

tailback   This is an offensive running back who is often the ball carrier because of his speed.

third down conversion   On a third down, the offense successfully moves the ball the full ten yards required to get a new first down. Getting a lot of third down conversions indicates that the offense is moving and controlling the ball effectively.

thrown for a loss   This is the same as *tackled for a loss.*

tight end   This is an offensive receiver who is on the line of scrimmage next to the offensive linemen at the beginning of a play. The tight end usually does more blocking than receiving, but he is an eligible receiver.

time of possession   The time of possession indicates the amount of time during the game that the offense had possession of the ball.

touchback   A touchback occurs when the ball is punted into the end zone and ruled as "dead." It also occurs when the punt receiver catches the ball in the end zone and downs the ball by putting his knee down. The ball is moved out to the 20-yard line to begin the next play.

touchdown   A touchdown occurs when an offensive player with the ball gets into the end zone to score six points. The ball, while in the possession of a player who is in bounds, crosses over the plane of the goal line. The ball, not necessarily the player, must be over the goal line. A touchdown also occurs when the ball is caught by a receiver already in the end zone.

turnover   A fumble or an interception turns the ball over to the other team. The offense loses the ball.

two-minute drill   This term refers to the accelerated plays that occur when only two minutes are left in the half. This is the time when a hurry-up offense is used.

two-minute warning   This official timeout indicates that only two minutes remain in the half. Teams often play more accelerated and more aggressively when only two minutes in the half remain.

two-point conversion   The offense attempts to score two points instead of kicking for one point after a touchdown. An offensive player needs to get the ball into the end zone. The ball may be carried across the goal line or thrown to a receiver who catches the ball in the end zone.

unnecessary roughness   This is a personal foul for any type of unnecessary roughness toward another player. Tackling a ball carrier after he is unquestionably out of bounds or intentionally kicking or striking another player are examples of unnecessary roughness. This infraction results in a fifteen yard penalty.

unsportsmanlike conduct   This is a type of personal foul that can include any type of behavior that shows lack of sportsmanlike conduct such as taunting players on the opposing team, using abusive language and gestures, and making contact with an official.

weak side   This term refers to the side of the offensive line that does not have the tight end.

wedge   A wedge is an offensive blocking strategy in which blockers form a V-shaped "wall" in front of a kick returner so the kick returner can run far and long with the ball. The wedge is designed to keep the oncoming players from disrupting the path of the kick returner.

wide receiver   The wide receiver is an offensive player who runs down the field to catch passes.

wide out   This is another name for the wide receiver.

Will   This is a nickname for the weak outside linebacker, who is positioned on the side of the field that does not have the tight end.

zone coverage   This is a defensive strategy in which defensive players are assigned to cover a specific section of the field, rather than to cover specific players.